AF516298

KIDSOURCE

SCIENCE EXPERIMENTS

By Amy Hansen
Illustrated by Mike Moran

Viva Books Private Limited
New Delhi • Mumbai • Chennai • Kolkata • Bangalore

Copyright © NTC/Contemporary Publishing Group, USA

First South Asian Edition 2000

VIVA BOOKS PRIVATE LIMITED

- 4262/3 Ansari Road, Daryaganj, New Delhi 110 002
  E-mail: viva@vivagroupindia.net
- 215-216 New Apollo Estate, 2nd Floor, Mogra Lane, Andheri (E), Mumbai 400 069
  E-mail: vivamumbai@vivagroupindia.net
- 7 Aziz Mulk, Seventh Street, Thousand Lights, Chennai 600 006
  E-mail: vivachennai@vivagroupindia.net
- B–103, Jindal Towers, 21/1A/3, Darga Road, Kolkata 700 017
  E-mail: vivakolkata@vivagroupindia.net
- 7 Sovereign Park Apts., 56-58 K. R. Road, Basavanagudi, Bangalore 560 004
  Email: vivabangalore@vivagroupindia.net

Published by arrangement with:

NTC/Contemporary Publishing Group,
4255 West Touhy Avenue, Lincolnwood (Chicago), Illinois 60646-1975, USA

All rights reserved. No part of this book may be reproduced or transmitted in any form or by any means without permission from the publishers.

This edition is licensed for sale in India, Bangladesh, Nepal, Pakistan and Sri Lanka only. Not for export elsewhere.

ISBN 81-7649-164-0

Published by Vinod Vasishtha for Viva Books Private Limited, 4262/3 Ansari Road, Daryaganj, New Delhi 110 002 and printed at Rajkamal Electric Press, B35/9 G T Karnal Road, Delhi 110 033.

CONTENTS

ACKNOWLEDGMENTS

This book would not have been possible without the help of many people. I'd like to thank the following for their contributions: Theodore Antonakos and the 1998–99 Takoma Park Middle School Science Club, the scientists interviewed throughout this book, and my friends and family, including my parents, Anne and Steven Hansen; my brother, Hugh Hansen, who is also a physics teacher; Terry Savage, writer and mother; and Marcia Clemmitt, writer and teacher. Most especially, I'd like to thank my husband, Bobby, and my son, Scott, who experimented with enthusiasm. Thank you all!

INTRODUCTION

Are you fascinated by the world around you—rocks, plants, animals, the air, the ocean? Do you enjoy grouping things together, like insects or seashells? When you tackle your homework, do you do it in a logical, organized way? Do you like to ask questions, questions, and more questions? Then you've got all the makings of a scientist.

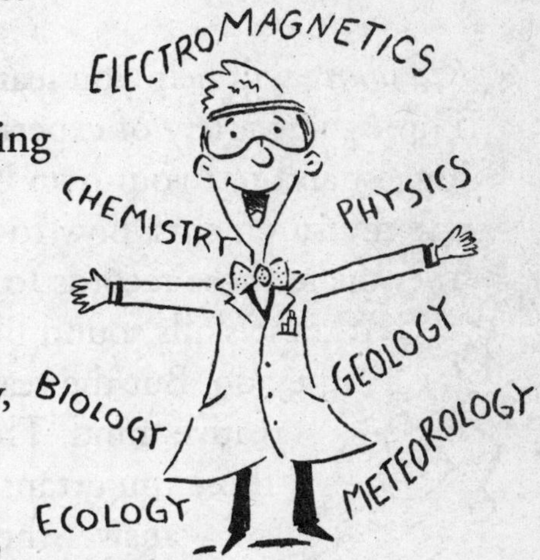

The experiments in *KidSource* cover a variety of scientific fields. Each field is a different way of exploring our world and the whole universe. Because science involves such a wide area of knowledge, a scientist chooses a particular branch in which to specialize. Chapters 3 through 9 in this book each cover one of these branches: biology, geology, meteorology, ecology, chemistry, and physics. Electromagnetics is a part of physics, but it's cool enough to get its own chapter.

Want to make quicksand? Go to page 73. Ready to create your own fruit fly farm? Turn to page 23. You don't need to read this book from front to back. Find the experiments that interest you the most and dive right in, then try out the others.

KidSource contains two types of fun and fascinating experiments: Six-Minute Science projects, and the more complex Experiments. Before you start each project, read through the Background, Materials, and Procedure sections, and make sure you have all your materials and equipment together.

At the end of the experiment, "What's Going On?" explains what happened and why. To go a step further, read the section called "Want to Do More?" Some of the skills you learn in one experiment can be used in others. You'll also find that the different sciences themselves overlap. The sidebars throughout this book provide fun and historical facts as well as tips on doing the experiments. In addition, key terms have been highlighted in **bold**. They're defined in the glossary at the back of the book.

CHAPTER 1

TESTING...TESTING...

The most beautiful thing we can experience is the mysterious. It is the source of all true art and science.

Albert Einstein, physicist, 1930

KidSource will help you learn how to be a scientist. Through a variety of experiments, you'll learn how to suggest and test your own hypotheses, how to take accurate measurements, how to keep detailed records, and how to evaluate those records to find the answers you're seeking.

If these skills sound like they take a lot of discipline, well, they do. But the real heart of science lies in having a creative mind. That's what scientists need to think of all those important questions and come up with theories to answer those questions. So if you enjoy thinking of new ideas and new ways of doing things, you're in the right field. After doing the experiments in this book and then coming up with some on your own, you'll see that science is a fun way to get those creative juices flowing.

THE SCIENTIFIC METHOD

When scientists try to find answers to those burning questions, they don't just jump right in and start experimenting. To get the best results, they follow an established procedure of investigation called the *scientific method.* Here's how it works.

The first step is *observation.* When you look at the world around you, what do you see, hear, smell, feel, and taste? How would you describe it? To be a scientist, you must learn to be a sharp observer and gather information. You must notice things without having them pointed out to you. For example, when you walked into class today, were any of the overhead lights burned out? You may not have thought to look.

After making an observation, you come up with a *question*. Why does what you observe work the way it does? What makes the sky blue? Why does a snake flick its tongue in and out?

The third step is to form a ***hypothesis***. A hypothesis is a possible answer to your question. More correctly, it is an educated guess. You create it by using all the information you have gathered from your observations, along with information collected from reading books and magazines or talking with scientific experts.

Once your hypothesis is in place, you *test* it. This is the most fun and exciting step for a lot of people. In this book, the testing is done mostly through experiments. An experiment is performed in a controlled environment, which is a space created by humans, such as a laboratory.

Two other testing methods are field studies and modeling. In a field study, researchers observe how a subject behaves in the wild instead of in the lab. An example would be biologists studying mountain gorillas in their native African habitat. Modeling is used for subjects that are too big to handle. For example, would a black hole fit inside a lab? Of course not. Scientists must instead simulate, or create an imitation of, a black hole.

THINGS AREN'T ALWAYS WHAT THEY SEEM

The Greek philosopher Aristotle thought he knew how the Earth worked. To him, it was logical that heavier objects fall faster than lighter objects. Aristotle never tested his theory, however. He just assumed it was correct. Nearly 2,000 years later, Italian astronomer and physicist Galileo wanted to test scientific theories instead of just accepting them as fact. In testing Aristotle's theory, he found that light and heavy objects fall at the same rate. To everyone's surprise, Aristotle had been wrong! On Earth, some objects, such as feathers, "stay up" longer than others because they are held up by air resistance. **But on the Moon, where there is no atmosphere and no air resistance, a feather and a bowling ball will fall at the same speed.**

After the testing is done, you draw a conclusion based on your analysis of the test results. Was your hypothesis correct? Did you answer your original question?

Finally, as a scientist you can communicate your findings to the public. This is an important part of the scientific process. Scientists publish their findings in journals and present them to their fellow scientists at conferences. From these results, other scientists form new questions, and the process starts all over again.

WHY EXPERIMENT?

Galileo proved that theories have to be tested (see sidebar on page 7). In fact, scientists test and retest their hypotheses until there is as little doubt as possible what the answer is. You may think all this testing and retesting is boring, but it isn't. It's like putting together pieces of a puzzle. One discovery leads to another.

Take what happened more than a century ago. In 1854, people in London were dying of cholera (KALL-er-uh). No one knew how the disease was being spread. A doctor named John Snow took a map of London and marked the location of every infected household. He then asked what these households had in common. Dr. Snow figured out that all of them drew their water from the same well. The disease was spreading through the water! When Londoners stopped using the well, the **epidemic** ended. Thanks to Dr. Snow, the science of *epidemiology* (ep-ih-dee-mee-OL-o-jee)—the study of how diseases are spread—took a giant leap forward.

Cholera still occurs around the world, but because of Dr. Snow's work, we know it always travels in water. Modern-day researchers use advanced techniques to track cholera. Satellite pictures taken from outer space are used to track the microscopic bacteria that cause the disease. Cholera bacteria are found among tiny plants, called plankton, in the ocean. Plankton have blooms that are bright enough to show up on satellite pictures. When a bloom is spotted, the people in the area are warned to purify their drinking water. Someday, someone will use this knowledge to find a way to wipe out cholera for good.

You'll see for yourself how scientific knowledge builds on itself by working through the experiments in this book. After doing the initial experiment, the section called "Want to Do More?" expands on the information that you already have.

CHAPTER 2

THE BASICS

I love fools' experiments. I am always making them.

Charles Darwin, naturalist, 1887

Before you pull on that white lab coat and dive into the experiments that follow, you must know the basics. First, you need to be prepared with all the right tools and guidelines. Second, you need to know the different ways to manage the information, or data, you'll be collecting. After you've done some or all of the experiments, you might like to try and come up with your own.

PLAYING IT SAFE

Scientists work hard to stay safe—especially when their experiments can be dangerous—and so should you.

- Always get permission from a parent or other responsible adult before beginning an experiment. Make sure you have an adult to help you during any potentially dangerous steps, such as those that involve using a stovetop or going out to a lake.
- Read the instructions thoroughly before beginning each experiment. Gather all your materials and have them at hand. This will keep you from, say, leaving a hot stove unattended to go fetch that pail of dirt.
- Think about things you might need that *aren't* mentioned in the experiment. If you're going on a field trip, you'll need water, sunscreen, sunglasses, and sturdy walking shoes. Bring a companion, but if that's not possible, make sure your parent or older sibling knows where you're going and when you'll be back.

- If the chemicals you're using come in a container that says DANGER, believe it! Parental supervision is a must. Wear goggles when working with any kind of dangerous chemical.

- Wear an apron to protect your clothing. Keep your hair and clothing away from the experiment table. If you have long hair, tie it back. If you have long sleeves, roll them up. Remove any jewelry, particularly rings, bracelets, and long necklaces.
- Do not taste the material in the experiments.
- Keep your work area as clean as possible while you're doing the experiment, and clean up thoroughly when you're done.
- Don't mix your experiments with other projects. Wash your hands between projects.

THE RIGHT STUFF

Most of the equipment you'll be using can be found around the house or purchased at a store. The items below are used throughout the experiments in this book and should always be kept on hand:

- Measuring spoons and a measuring cup.
- Ruler or measuring tape.
- Your experiment notebook and a pen or pencil. Keep all your charts, observations, notes, and results together in your notebook.

You'll need a few other things that can be bought at a specialty store.

- From a gardening supply store, you'll need seeds.
- From a camera store, you can get thermometers for taking water temperature.
- From an electronics store, you can buy batteries and electrical wires.
- From a camping supply store, you'll need a compass.

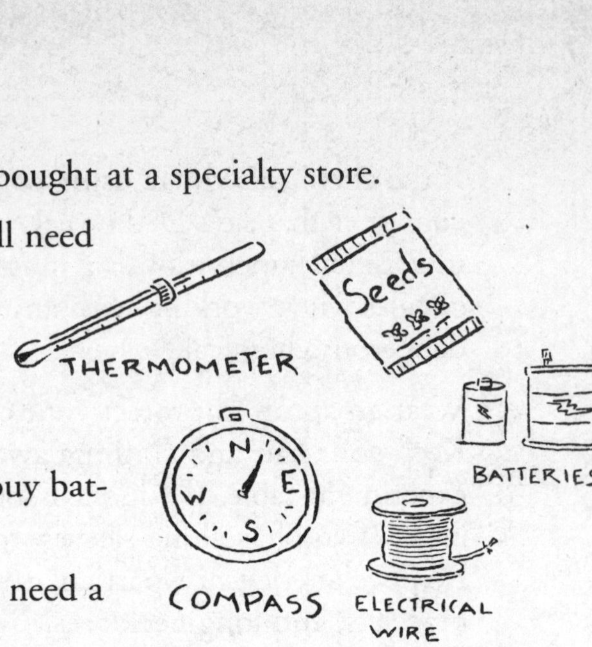

The above items are available at a scientific equipment store if you have one in your area. Check the Yellow Pages. You also can order this equipment from

Carolina Biological Supply
2700 York Rd.
Burlington, NC 27215
1-800-334-5551
☛ **http://www.carolina.com**

THEY WENT DATA-WAY

Data can come from observations. Sitting in the woods, for instance, you would observe different kinds of birds than you would if you are in an open field. But more often, data come in the form of measurements. You might measure the temperature of water in different containers. Or you might measure the speed that a toy car travels over various surfaces. How you keep track of your data and make sense of it later, called data management, depends on the type of information you collect and how you collect it.

LOG ENTRIES

Sometimes data are recorded and kept in a log. Your log is your experiment notebook. Every week or so you can complete a chart showing what you have observed and store it in your log. Out in the field, you can make sketches in your log of what you observe so you can look it up in a reference book later.

CHARTS

A chart comes in handy when you need to keep track of a lot of data. Charts are made of horizontal rows and vertical columns. This format lets you compare two parts of an experiment at the same time.

To set up a chart, you first need to determine how many variables, or elements, are in your experiment. Then, create the number of columns and rows you'll need. For example, if you are doing the "Plant Communities" experiment on page 59, you will have three variables, because there are three soil types. You would list the soil types in the first column. Next, you need to figure out what you are measuring. If you are measuring plant height each day for a week or more, you'd label the second column "Plant Height, Day 1," the third column "Plant Height, Day 2," and so on. Sometimes scientists add a column titled "Other" to record unexpected observations.

GRAPHS

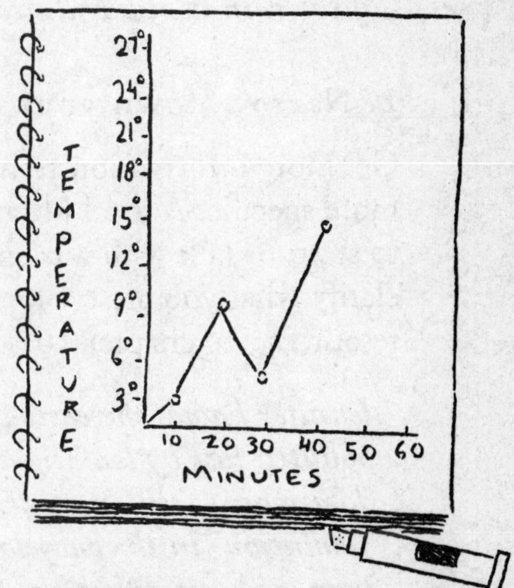

Data recorded in a chart can then be displayed in a graph. In the "Black and White" experiment on page 84, you are comparing the heat absorption rates of white and black cans. You would create a graph comparing the rise in temperature with the time it took to do so.

A graph consists of an X axis (horizontal line) and a Y axis (vertical line). Together they form a capital L. The starting point is where the two axes meet. You would make an equally spaced dot or hatch mark every 10 minutes, or however frequently you record the temperature. The minutes follow the X axis, and the temperatures follow the Y axis. Once you have put in all the dots or marks from your readings, connect them to show the temperature progression of the cans.

DESIGN YOUR OWN EXPERIMENT

Want to do your own experiment? Need help setting it up? Follow the steps below. We've provided Jennifer's story as an example.

1. Come up with an idea or question.

Look around you. What do you wonder about in your very own backyard, or in the world at large? What do you want to know more about? Think about the experiments you've done so far. What questions have they left unanswered?

Jennifer, a seventh grader, finishes the Six-Minute Science project on air pollution ("The Air Up There," page 64) and wonders if the rain is also polluted.

2. Narrow down your question.

Get more information to make your question more specific. A local library is a good place to start; or talk with a friend or a parent to clarify what you are trying to ask. For other resources, see chapter 10.

Jennifer knows she can't tell if the rain is polluted just by looking at it. She needs to do a more specific test. Jennifer looks up "Pollution" in the encyclopedia and sees the term acid rain. *Now she has a more specific question: "Is there acid rain in my area?"*

KIDSOURCE TIPS

Keeping track of what is in each container you use is an important part of your experiment. Make labels by writing the name of the substance on pieces of masking tape. Use a permanent marker so your writing won't get washed or rubbed off. Stick the pieces of tape on the containers. If you don't have masking tape, write on a piece of paper and attach it with clear tape.

3. Write a hypothesis.

Now, write out a hypothesis in your experiment notebook. You can revise it as you continue to design the experiment, but it's important to get it down now. The hypothesis can be as straightforward as putting the question you asked in statement form. The usual method, however, is to write the negative answer to your question, or null hypothesis. Then you perform your experiments to try and disprove it.

Jennifer writes out the null hypothesis: "There is no acid rain in my area."

4. Find the right test.

How will you set up your test? You may need to do more research in science books to learn about testing methods.

Jennifer decides she needs to test for acidity levels in the rainwater. She performs the experiment "Are You an Acid?" (page 68) and learns how to tell acids from bases.

5. Design your experiment.

Do this part step by step, and you should end up with a good test.

- Determine the **variables** (such as type of material, time of day, and amount of material).
- Decide which variables you will change. How will you change them?
- Decide which variables will remain constant.
- Create a **control group**.
- Decide how many observations you will need to get a representative result. Read the KidSource Tips on duplication (page 61) and averaging (page 83) for more details.
- Get the equipment needed for the experiment.

- Decide how you will keep track of the results. Will you use charts, graphs, or another method?
- Can this experiment be replicated, or done again? A good experiment can be repeated by someone else so your results can be verified.

Jennifer's variables are the amount of rain that falls, the time of day it falls, the time of year it falls, her geographic location, and the rainwater itself. Jennifer doesn't know if rain might be more or less acidic if a lot or a little falls. She also doesn't know if there might be a difference if the rain falls in the morning or at night, or in spring versus summer. She can't control the rain, but she can keep records of where and when she collects her samples.

From the "Are You an Acid?" experiment, Jennifer knows that unpolluted water has a pH of 5.6 and uses that as her control group. She decides to take three samples during the next rainstorm, and creates a chart to record the test results of each sample.

6. Perform the experiment.

You're ready! Be sure to keep a record of your findings.

When the rain comes, Jennifer places three clean jars in the backyard. After the rain stops, she picks up her samples. She finds she can hold only two jars at a time, and her dog knocks the third one over. Now she's down to two samples, but she will still be able to complete the experiment.

7. Write up your results.

When you've completed the experiment, write down what you've observed. Organize your data in the format you've chosen.

Jennifer records the results of her rainwater samples on a chart. Each one is slightly acidic, but not more acidic than the control water.

8. Draw a conclusion and communicate your results.

Did you find out if your hypothesis was true or false? Did you find out anything else? Tell your results to your family, friends, or classmates. Remember, science builds on itself.

Jennifer decides that for that evening, there was no acid rain falling in her area. The null hypothesis she wrote out was true.

9. Come up with new questions.

Think over the results of your experiment. You may find that your answer opens up a whole new set of questions.

Jennifer had heard that acid rain was eating away at some of the statues in a nearby town, so her results surprised her. She decides to do the test again next time it rains. She also decides to go to the library to find out if acid rain is worse at different times of the year.

KIDSOURCE TIPS

Don't jump right into your experiment. Think things through first. Does it involve something you can observe—that is, something you can see, hear, smell, touch, or feel? Can you take measurements? Do you have the correct materials and know how to use them? When you design an experiment, you are creating an investigation from beginning to end. If it is too complicated, you may never get to the finish line.

The Accidental Discovery

In 1928, Dr. Alexander Fleming was studying bacteria that cause diseases, diseases he wanted to prevent. As the good doctor checked the samples in the petri dishes, all systems were go, except for one dish—which, to his surprise, had a spot of mold growing in it. Dr. Fleming hadn't planned to grow mold. But instead of throwing out that sample, he took a closer look at it. Under the microscope, he saw that all around the mold, the bacteria were dying!

Excitedly, Dr. Fleming began growing and testing more of this mold, which was called *Penicillium notatum*. He recorded his experiments carefully. Dr. Fleming hoped the mold would prove to be a way to stop bacterial infections before they started, but the mold didn't do what he wanted it to do. Frustrated, he ended his experiments without learning the mold's true importance.

Ten years later, Drs. Howard Florey and Ernst Chain picked up from where Dr. Fleming left off. Working from his records, they isolated the substance in the mold that kills bacteria and called it penicillin. Since then, penicillin has become one of the most important drugs in medical history.

You've probably seen mold on bread before (if not, do the "Good as Mold" experiment on page 33). Mold spores grow in warm, damp conditions and are too small to see individually, but when there are a lot of them, they show up as splashes of green, blue, or yellow.

BIOLOGY

Bacteria make digestion possible. Fungi give us penicillin and other medicines. "Squirmies" such as worms and termites are nature's recyclers. It's the tiny species that really run the planet.

Thomas Lovejoy, ecologist, 1990

A certain type of alga lives frozen in the Antarctic where no other life-forms can survive. Tubeworms with bright red plumes have been discovered thousands of feet below the surface of the ocean. And we human beings are pretty amazing creatures, too.

LIFE AS WE KNOW IT

Biology is the study of life. And there probably is no better place to study it than here on Earth. Our planet is teeming with millions of different types of life. Take breathing, for instance: Fish use their gills to push water filled with oxygen past their lungs. We use our noses to suck in air filled with oxygen into our lungs. Some forms of life are *anaerobic* (an-eh-ROH-bik)—they don't need any oxygen at all.

Despite these differences, all life-forms have many of the same goals. We all need energy, which we get through eating (if you're a mammal), through **photosynthesis** (if you're a plant), or **chemosynthesis** (if you're a bacterium). We breathe (though not all of us breathe oxygen). We use water. We grow. We reproduce. We die.

Animals, plants, fungi, slime molds, algae, bacteria, viruses—all living organisms adapt to the world in which they live. As you perform the experiments in this chapter, think about what plants, animals, and fungi need. What do their ways of adapting tell you about how and where they live? Getting an answer is not always easy.

You can't just pretend you're a turtle and blend right in. You must have the right tools.

Biologists also use a classification system, which organizes life-forms into categories from very broad to very small: kingdom, phylum, class, order, family, genus, and species. Humans are members of the Hominidae family (which also includes apes and monkeys), the genus *Homo,* and the species *sapiens* (meaning wise and intelligent).

In the experiments that follow, you'll be examining several ways in which life has adapted.

Experiment
Balloon Magic

Background:

Yeast is used to make bread rise. The more yeast eats and grows, the more gas it makes. Which food does yeast like best? Find out in this experiment.

Materials:

- two empty, clean 16-ounce plastic soda bottles
- two balloons large enough to fit over the mouth of a soda bottle
- two glasses
- one package yeast (make sure to check the expiration date)
- wooden spoon
- sugar
- funnel
- vinegar
- masking tape and pen for labeling

Procedure:

1. Stretch out each balloon by blowing it up, then letting the air out. Stretch them again with your hands.
2. In one glass, mix the yeast with 2 cups warm water. This is your yeast mixture. Let it sit until the yeast starts to bubble.
3. Stir the mixture gently with the spoon. Pour 1 cup of it into the second glass. Add 2 tablespoons sugar to the second glass.
4. Using the funnel, pour the mixture from the second glass into one of the soda bottles. Stretch the balloon over the mouth of the bottle as shown. Wash out the empty glass and funnel.

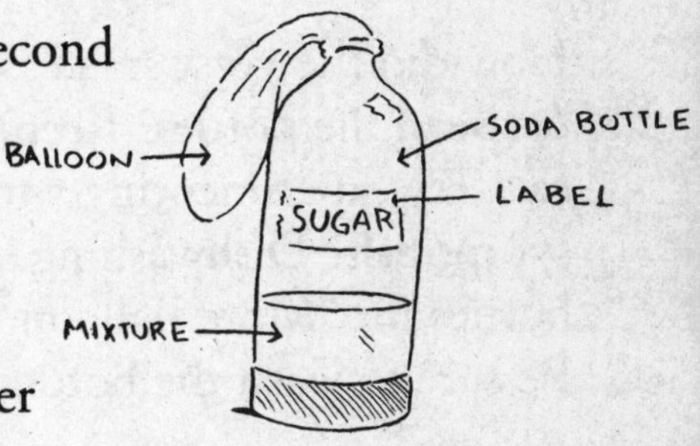

5. Add 2 tablespoons vinegar to the remaining yeast mixture, then repeat step 4 using the other soda bottle.
6. Label the first bottle "Sugar" and the other "Vinegar."
7. Place both bottles in a dark, warm (not hot) area. Over the next two hours, the yeast should bubble and grow, filling the balloons with gas. Before the time is up, guess which bottle will have the bigger balloon. Write down your hypothesis in your experiment notebook. For example, "When I feed yeast (sugar/vinegar), the yeast will grow the most."
8. Check the bottles every 15 minutes, picking up each and gently swishing the liquid. Each time you check, measure the circumference (the distance around the outside) of the fattest part of each balloon. To do this, wrap your measuring tape around the balloon. You also can use a string and ruler. Write down the measurement.
9. Create a chart in your experiment notebook. Make two horizontal columns for the sugar and vinegar. Make a vertical column for each 15-minute measurement. Record your measurements on the chart.

What's Going On?

The sugar bottle should have the bigger balloon. Yeast contains lots of fungi, which hibernate when the environment is cold and dry. But when they are in a warm environment, yeast grows rapidly.

Yeast cannot make its own food. Instead, it breaks down the food around it to create energy to eat. This process, called fermentation, produces carbon dioxide—the bubbles—and alcohol. We use the bubbles for baking bread and for making beer and wine.

Want to Do More?

How did the yeast smell? What did it look like? Could you see any difference between the bottles? Keep track of your observations. What else does yeast eat? Try experimenting with different possibilities. Would it eat flour? Corn syrup? Salt? Dishwashing soap? You may want to save your balloons and soda bottles for "More Balloon Magic" in the chemistry chapter (pages 76 and 77). Be sure to wash the bottles out thoroughly.

Experiment
Fruit Fly Farm

Background:

Wherever there is rotting fruit, there probably will be fruit flies. Where did these insects come from? Were the fruit fly eggs already on the fruit, or did they come from somewhere else?

Materials:

- two pieces rotting fruit (melons or pears work well)
- two empty glass jars
- two wet paper towels
- plastic wrap
- two rubber bands that fit securely over the necks of the jars
- funnel
- magnifying glass

Procedure:

1. Outdoors, put a piece of fruit inside each jar.
2. Place a wet paper towel inside each jar. This will be the flies' water supply.
3. Cover the top of one jar with plastic wrap and secure it with a rubber band. This will be your "covered" jar.
4. Cover the top of the other jar with plastic wrap. Poke the funnel through the plastic to make a hole as shown. Secure the plastic with a rubber band.

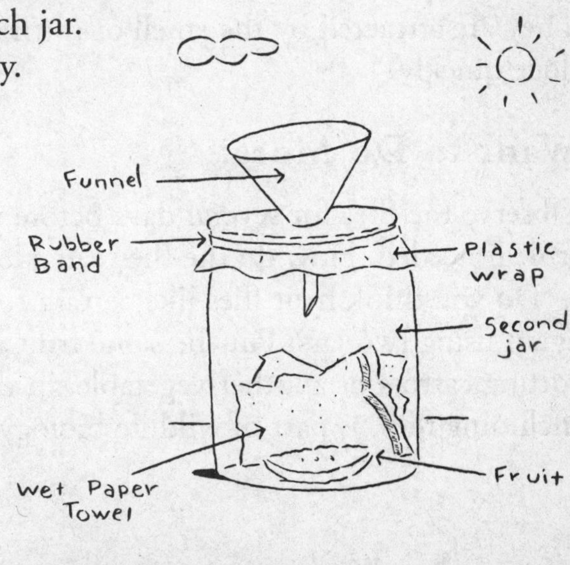

This will be your "uncovered" jar. If the fruit flies enter from the outside, they will not be able to get out.

5. Write down your hypothesis in your experiment notebook. For example, "I think the fruit flies will appear in the jar that is (covered/uncovered)."
6. Leave the jars in a safe, sunny place (preferably outdoors) for about a week. Check them daily and record any changes in your notebook.
7. When you see the fruit flies, study them for a day or two with the magnifying glass. Draw one of the flies in your notebook.
8. When you feel you have examined them thoroughly, take off the plastic and let the flies out. Fruit flies have a short life span and die within a few days without food. Be sure to wash out the jars before recycling or reusing them.

What's Going On?

You have set up a **controlled experiment**. If the fruit fly eggs are already inside the fruit, they will not be able to get out of the first jar. If the fruit flies come from the outside, they will not be able to escape after entering through the hole in the second jar.

Your experiment should have found that fruit flies come from the outside. They are attracted by the smell of rotting food. Once they find it, they reproduce quickly.

Want to Do More?

Observe the flies for several days before you let them go. Add more water or fruit if needed. How do the flies eat? How do they lay eggs?

Do you think fruit flies like certain foods? Set up a second experiment, again using two jars. Put the same fruit in one jar and stale bread or pasta, or rotting carrots or another vegetable, in the other jar. Observing animals, including flies, is part of wildlife biology.

Experiment
How Does Your Garden Grow? (Part 1)

Background:

We all know that plants grow roots down, stems up. But why do they grow like that? In this two-part experiment, you'll see if you can confuse first the roots, then the stems, into growing in a different direction.

Materials:

- packet of seeds (bean seeds work well, but any that are big enough to see will do)
- roll of paper towels
- eight clear plastic cups or empty glass jars
- masking tape and pen for labeling

Procedure:

1. Gather eight seeds. Save the packet (see the Kidsource Tip on page 27).
2. Tear off eight paper towels. Fold them in thirds to create eight long, narrow strips. Wet each towel with water until they are damp but not sopping wet.
3. Place a seed at the end of each towel as shown. Roll up the towel around the seed as you would roll up a sleeping bag. Fold the edges under.
4. Place each towel, end first, inside a cup. Arrange the cups into four groups of two cups each. Label the groups 1, 2, 3, and 4.

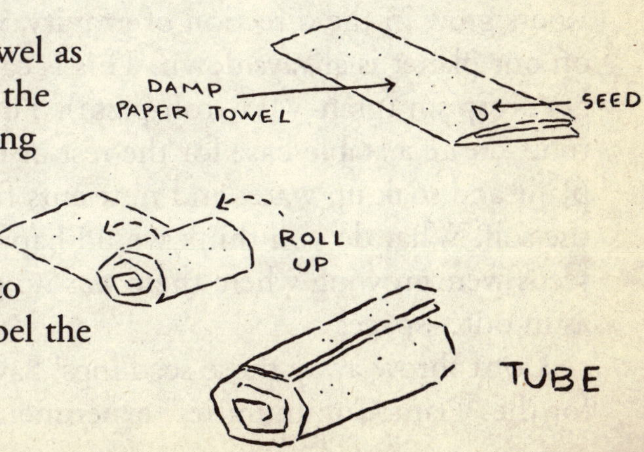

5. In a few days, your seeds should start sending out roots. You will need to unwrap the towels gently to see this. After you see the roots, rewrap the seedlings and rewet the towels.
6. To get the roots to grow differently, leave group 1 with the roots pointing down. This is your control group. Turn the two towels in group 2 horizontal so that the roots are pointed sideways. Turn the towels in group 3 upside down. Crumple up each towel in group 4.
7. What do you think will happen? Write out your hypothesis in your experiment notebook. For example: "The roots in group 2 will grow (out/down/up)."
8. Create a table in your experiment notebook. You will need five columns, one for the date and one for each group of cups. Whenever you check the seedlings, record the date and any observations you made. Write down the direction of the roots, how long it took them to start growing that way, if the stems are starting to show, and anything else you find interesting.
9. Check the seedlings and roots every other day for a week. What has happened?

What's Going On?

You should have found that the roots of all the seedlings eventually grow pointing down. Roots grow in the direction of **gravity,** which on our planet is always down. This is called gravitropism (grah-VIH-troh-pizm). The roots create a stable base for the rest of the plant and soak up water and nutrients from the soil. What do you think would happen if the seeds were growing where there was no gravity, such as in outer space?

Don't throw away those seedlings! Save them for Part 2 and for the "Plant Communities" experiment on page 59.

KIDSOURCE TIPS

Read the instructions on the seed packet. If your backyard has a garden and it is a good time of year for growing plants outdoors, you can plant the seedling. Dig a hole in the soil that is slightly deeper than the roots of the seedling. Place the plant in the hole. Fill it in with enough dirt so that the plant can stand up on its own.

You also can grow your seedlings indoors. At a gardening store, buy gravel, potting soil, and a pot big enough for an adult plant. Put the gravel in the bottom of the pot. Pour some soil on top. Gently place your seedling into the pot and add enough dirt so that the plant is supported and can stand on its own. Water it right away, and afterward as needed.

Experiment

How Does Your Garden Grow? (Part 2)

Background:

If roots always grow down, as you found in Part 1 of this experiment, why do stems always grow upward? In Part 2, you will try to get a seedling to grow differently by creating a maze for it. Will a plant still grow upward if its light source is moved sideways? This experiment should be done after at least one of the seeds in Part 1 has sprouted roots.

Materials:

- small, growing plant from Part 1, or any small purchased plant with vines
- cardboard box with dividers used to ship bottles (available at a grocery or liquor store)
- scissors
- paper bag
- masking tape and duct tape

Procedure:

1. If you are using a seedling from Part 1, plant it in a small container of dirt; the plastic pots that seedlings are sold in work well. Wait a few days to make sure the seedling continues to grow. If you are using a purchased plant, make sure the pot is small enough to fit inside the cardboard box.

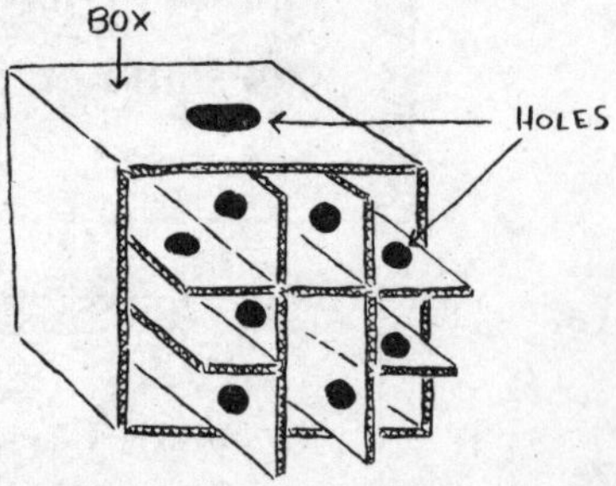

2. Turn the box on its side and pull out the dividers. Create a simple maze by cutting holes in the dividers as shown. Cut a hole in the top of the box so that light can get in. Make sure the maze does not double back on itself and that it connects to the hole.

3. Place the plant on the bottom of the box at the start of the maze.

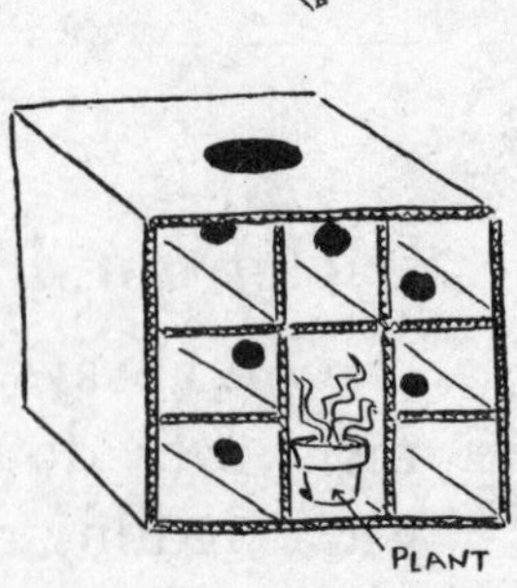

4. Cover the open side with the paper bag and tape it in place as shown. You will have to cut the bag to fit. Use masking tape, because you will need to untape and retape.

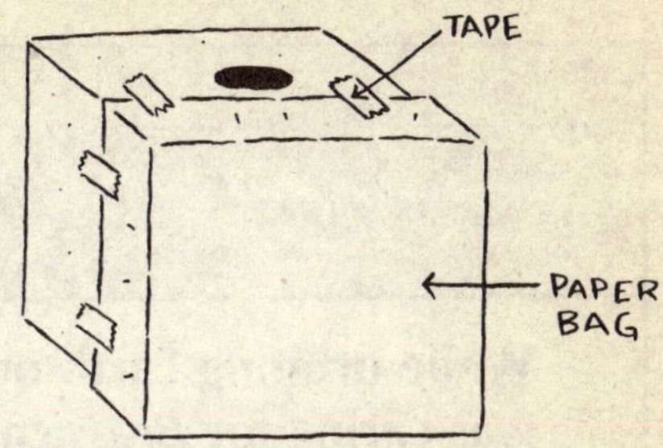

5. Cover up any other holes in the box (except the one on top) with duct tape to block out light. Place the box by a window so that light can get in through the top.
6. In your experiment notebook, create a chart showing the day and location of the plant for two weeks.
7. What do you think will happen? Write down your hypothesis.
8. Remove the paper bag every other day to measure and record your plant's progress. Water the plant if needed, then re-cover the box.

What's Going On?

Plants need light to produce food and are programmed to seek that light. This is called phototropism (foh-TUH-troh-pizm). Your plant wove its way through the maze until it found the source of light. What happened to the plant as it did this? Besides the bends in the stem, did your plant look different from other plants you've seen?

If the light source doesn't come from directly above, the plant will move accordingly. Try the experiment again with another seedling, this time turning the box so that the hole is on the side. Although there are no cardboard mazes in nature, phototropism is all around us. If you've ever seen a row of sunflowers, you'll notice they are turned east to catch the first rays of sun in the morning.

A MATTER OF GRAVITY

While orbiting Earth on the Mir space station, astronaut Mike Foale was caring for *Brassica rapa* seeds. The seeds had sprouted, but in nearly zero gravity the plants did not know which way to grow. Some stems were growing downward, others straight out. The roots were snaking up or sideways.

Back on Earth, Dr. Mary Musgrave of Louisiana State University suggested that the plants be given more light, and they began to grow normally. Now Dr. Musgrave wondered whether the seedlings would flower and produce more seeds. Plants absorb carbon dioxide from the air. Light, warm air rises and heavy, cold air falls. On Mir, however, the air did not move because there is no gravity to pull the cold air down. And the warm air didn't rise because in space it isn't lighter than anything else. The plants on Mir couldn't get enough carbon dioxide.

Dr. Musgrave had the plants moved to the space station's open living quarters, where the air was constantly moving. The plants soon flowered and produced so many seeds that Foale was able to plant those seeds and do the experiment again. That's good news for future space travel, says Dr. Musgrave, because astronauts need plants for food and to reproduce oxygen.

Experiment
Match Game

Background:

You may like to stay up late, but humans actually are not nocturnal creatures. Things we can do easily in daylight are almost impossible to do at night. For instance, can you match up colors, say black with black or blue with blue? Easy as pie in the daytime, but just try it in the dark!

Materials:

- one sheet each of dark blue and black construction paper
- scissors
- bowl
- five paper clips

Procedure:

1. Cut both sheets of construction paper to make ten pieces of each color, all about the same size. Put the pieces into the bowl and mix the colors together.
2. Take the bowl and paper clips and go into a semidark room. It should be as dark as a night that has a few stars out, but not pitch-black so that you can't see anything. Wait a few minutes. Once your eyes have adjusted, look around the room. You should be able to barely see the outlines of any furniture. If there is still too much light, put a towel across the bottom of the door, or find another room.

3. Take the pieces of paper out of the bowl and match black with black, and blue with blue. Fasten each pair together with a paper clip.
4. When you're done, turn on the light and check your work. Your matches weren't all perfect, were they?

What's Going On?

Our eyes have two different ways of seeing, one for daytime and one for night. When you are in a lighted area, the pupil (the black dot in the center of your eye) gets very small, letting in only a small amount of light. Behind the pupil is a kind of screen called the retina (RET-in-uh). Inside the retina are two types of light-sensitive nerve cells, one called cones and one called rods.

Cones work in light. They detect colors and small details. Most of the cones are located directly behind the pupil. Rods work in semidarkness. They can see dim lights and shapes but cannot identify colors or make out details. Rods are located all over your eye. At night, this makes your peripheral (puh-RIF-er-ul) vision (your ability to see to the side, above, and below when you are staring straight ahead) almost as good as your central, or straight-ahead, vision.

Want to Do More?

When you sorted the pieces of paper, you were asking the rods to do the cones' work: identifying colors. Now ask the cones to do the rods' work: seeing shapes in the dark. Go back into the semidark room and keep your eyes open as you turn off the lights. What can you see? Now close your eyes and wait a couple of minutes. Open your eyes. Things should be more visible because your night vision has taken over.

Experiment
Good as Mold

Background:

Mold spores are all around us, but we can't see them unless they collect in large numbers. When they do, they appear in splotches of color—yellow, red, green, blue—and often are fuzzy looking. It's important to experiment with mold so you can recognize it when you see it on food.

Materials:

- slice of bread
- resealable plastic bag
- magnifying glass

Procedure:

1. Lay the bread on top of the plastic bag. Sprinkle about 12 drops of water on the bread.
2. Slide the bread into the plastic bag, but don't seal the bag.
3. Put the bread in a warm place. A kitchen cabinet works well.
4. Check the bread after two days. If there is no mold, wait another two days. Commercially produced bread often contains preservatives, which slow down the mold's growth.
5. When your bread has splotches of color on it, seal the bag.
6. Examine the mold through the plastic. What color is it? What does it look like? Study the mold with a magnifying glass. Can you see the individual spores? Draw them in your experiment notebook. Write down your other observations.
7. When you are done, throw away the sealed bag.

What's Going On?

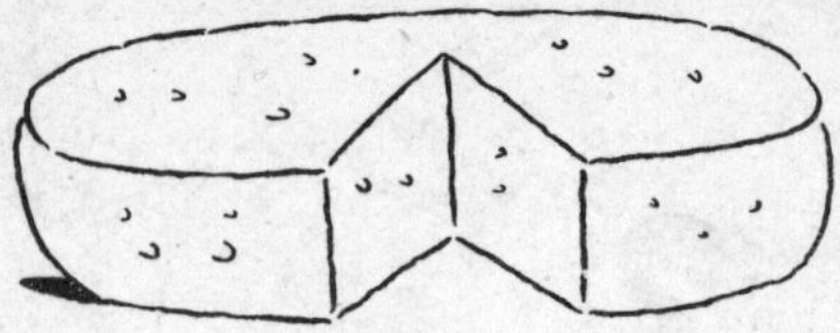

Mold spores float through the air. They land everywhere, but they grow only where conditions are favorable. Mold needs moisture, food, and heat to grow. Your damp, warm piece of bread provides the perfect place.

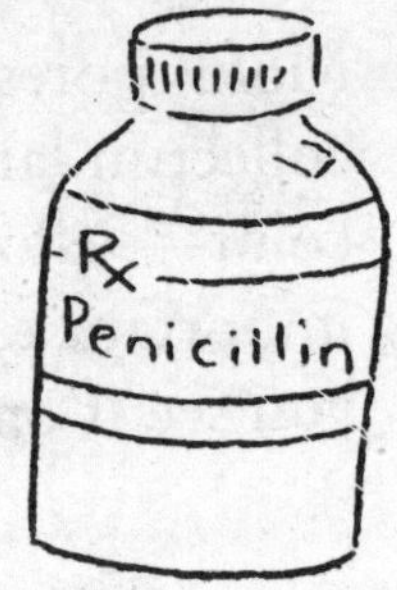

Some molds make food taste bad, but others are beneficial. Molds are used to make medicines such as penicillin, and they are used in certain cheeses. Believe it or not, that cheese you like tastes good because of mold!

Want to Do More?

What other variables might affect mold growth? Try leaving a slice of bread in direct sunlight, another inside a covered box, and another inside the refrigerator. Remember to dampen the bread with water first. Does the mold prefer one type of bread over another? Do you get different-colored molds with different types of bread?

GEOLOGY

Ultimately … the forces which move hundreds of millions of tons of silt and half a trillion tons of water annually … are too powerful to contain.

Michael Parfit, writing about the Mississippi River in *Smithsonian* magazine, February 1993

Outside the small town of Amherst, Ohio, lies a large limestone quarry (KWAR-ee)—a place where stone is excavated. To the townspeople, this means they have a ready supply of building material. But to geologists, the limestone means this part of Ohio was once underwater!

Limestone is formed when millions of seashells, left behind from dried lakes or oceans, pile up on top of each other. As the pile becomes higher and higher, the weight presses the shells into a solid, cream-colored mass. Because these are seashells, this means that wherever there are deposits of limestone, there was once water.

ROCKS 'N' ROLES

Geology is the study of the **Earth** and its origins. Geologists examine what's both on and below the Earth's surface to figure out how our 6.6-sextillion-ton planet works. If you cut open an onion, you will see that it is made of several layers. Our planet is like an onion. We live on the surface layer, called the *crust*. Below that is the *mantle*, and farther in are the *outer* and *inner cores*. All over the Earth, the crust varies from 4 to 44 miles thick. It is broken into sections called plates. Sometimes these plates shift and collide, creating mountains and causing earthquakes.

When geologists want to learn how our planet is formed, they look at the roles heat and pressure play inside the Earth and study the movement of the plates on which the continents lie. They also look at the forces that shape the Earth's surface, such as water, ice, and wind, which are powerful enough to move stone and rock. For example, scientists learned it was running water, not an earthquake, that created the Grand Canyon.

In this chapter, you will study the surface of our planet by observing rocks, the landscape around you, and the forces that change that landscape. As you examine different types of rock, try to imagine what the world was like when these rocks were formed.

Experiment
It's All Downhill from Here

Background:

When rain falls from the sky, the water is absorbed in some areas. But in other areas, the rain collects and creates mudslides. Why does this happen? In this experiment, you'll focus on how plants affect water flow and **erosion**.

Materials:

- newspapers
- trowel
- soil (from your backyard or purchased at a gardening store)
- three old cookie sheets
- sticks, leaves, and grass (from your backyard or a nearby park)
- two or three old books

Procedure:

1. This experiment gets messy. Spread newspapers over the table where you will be working, or work outdoors.

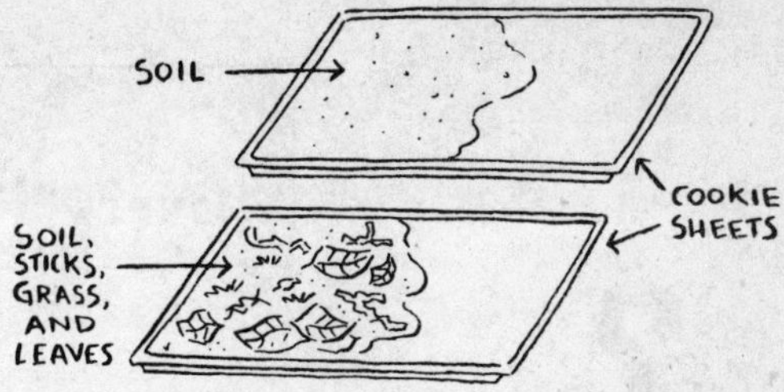

2. With the trowel, spread soil over about half of two cookie sheets.
3. Cover the soil on one sheet with sticks, grass, and leaves as shown. This will be your "forest" sheet. The other sheet will be your "non-vegetation" sheet.
4. Write out your hypothesis. For example: "I think the 'forest' cookie sheet (will have/will not have) the most erosion."

5. Prop up the soil ends of the two cookie sheets with two or three books as shown. Place the third cookie sheet under the opposite ends to catch the water. It's OK if the soil starts sliding down to the other end.
6. Pour a cup of water onto the two cookie sheets. Which lost more soil?

What's Going On?

Imagine you are sliding down a hill and trying to stop yourself. What would you do? You'd try to dig in your feet and grab on to something—a branch, a bush, a tree. It's the same when water runs downhill. If a tree gets in its way, the water slows down and soaks into it. If nothing is in its way, the water speeds up, mixing with and pushing more and more dirt aside to create a mudslide. This is one method of erosion.

Erosion occurs naturally when the flow of a river carves out more space for its riverbed, and when rain hits areas that are not covered with vegetation. Humans increase erosion through the clear-cutting of forests and other practices that remove natural vegetation.

Want to Do More?

Are there other ways of keeping water from washing away soil? Try building two hills of soil, one with a regular cone shape and the other with a spiral shape. Pour water down both. Even without vegetation, the spiral shape of the second hill helps slow down the water.

Experiment
Every Rock Tells a Story

Background:

You can tell where a rock came from just by looking at it. By starting a rock collection, you can determine if your area was once covered by water, or if volcanoes erupted there long ago. If you can find an outcropping—a place where **bedrock** sticks out of the ground—you can learn even more. Before you start, find out if a museum near you has rocks and minerals on display. Some museums have exhibits of local rocks, which will help you identify the rocks you find.

Materials:

- small resealable plastic bags
- field guide to rocks and minerals, available at a library
- masking tape and pen for labeling

Procedure:

1. Gather several rocks and place them in the plastic bags. Make sure you have permission if you are collecting rocks from someone else's property. Remember, don't remove rocks from parks. Use the field guide to see how many rocks you can identify.

2. In your experiment notebook, write descriptions of the rocks and what you think they are. If the rocks you found are in a park, write down where you found them so you can find them again.

3. Make labels for the rocks and place them on the bags.
4. Try to locate an outcropping in your area. You may need to call a state park and ask a park ranger. If you find one, ask a trusted adult to take you there. Be sure to bring your field guide and notebook.
5. Identify as many of the rocks in the outcropping as you can. You're likely to see large stripes of different colors. These are called sedimentary rocks. (See "Know Your Rocks" on page 42.)

What's Going On?

Much of the work in natural sciences is done through fieldwork and observation. The work isn't easy, but it is exciting. There is always the possibility that you will find something other scientists have overlooked!

Experiment
Sifting Through the Layers

Background:

Imagine that a storm is raging through your town. The usually calm river is filled with mud, pebbles, rocks, and even boulders. What will it look like when the storm is over?

Materials:

- a ramp (such as a piece of wood propped up by books) or the driveway of your house
- mud, sand, leaves, twigs
- stones of various sizes
- large mixing bowl
- wooden spoon
- hose (a watering can or pitcher also will work, but will have to be refilled)

Procedure:

1. Build your ramp. This experiment will get messy, so work outdoors.
2. Mix the mud, sand, leaves, twigs, and stones in the bowl, using the wooden spoon
3. Pour the mixture onto the top of the ramp. The ramp should not be so steep that the stones roll off. This will be your river model.

4. What do you think will happen when water is added? Which part of the mixture will wash away first? Write out your hypothesis of how you think the ingredients will end up (What will be on the bottom? What will be next? And so forth).
5. Pour water on the mixture to wash it away. Pour from only one direction to imitate a river coming through. What ended up on top?

What's Going On?

Your river separated the mixture by weight. The heavier material stayed near the top, and the lighter material washed downstream.

Rivers carry topsoil, sand, twigs, and leaves downstream. Farmers put their farmland at the end of a river so that they have a continuing supply of topsoil to grow crops. Good farmland is located alongside rivers as well. When a river floods and overflows its banks, it washes topsoil into the surrounding valley. Many farms in the United States and around the world are built in river floodplains because rivers supply fertile soil.

Want to Do More?

Make a model of a lake bed by pouring the mixture from this experiment into a jar and adding water. Shake it up. As the mixture settles, note what goes to the bottom first, then what goes next, and so on.

THE END OF THE WORLD

For years, scientists theorized that the dinosaurs became extinct because a meteor struck the Earth, but they lacked proof. In 1996, geologists digging in New Jersey found that proof in a layer of glass beads. Not the kind you use to make necklaces, but the kind that are formed after something huge hits the Earth—in this case, a meteor.

What's amazing is that this meteor actually struck thousands of miles away, in Mexico. It hit so hard that everything on the ground didn't just melt, it was vaporized—turned into gas—and formed a huge cloud. The impact produced so much energy that it propelled this cloud of vapor from Mexico all the way to New Jersey in about 10 minutes. Then the cloud started to rain. As the vapor fell, it cooled and formed solid glass beads, called spherules (SFEHR-ulz).

These beads were found about 1,260 feet underground. By examining this spot—called the Cretaceous-Tertiary boundary—the geologists knew the beads had formed between the Cretaceous (kreh-TAY-shus) period (the time of the dinosaurs) and the Tertiary (TER-shee-air-ee) period (the time of mammals). The ground below the beads was full of fossils, plankton (tiny plants and animals that float in water) that lived during the Cretaceous period. The ground above the beads contained only a few fossils, meaning that the plankton had been killed off.

The meteor that struck Earth at the end of the Cretaceous period—65 million years ago—wouldn't have killed off all the dinosaurs right away. But anything strong enough to move glass from Mexico to New Jersey in 10 minutes would have caused a lot of damage. Eventually the meteor brought about the end of the world as the dinosaurs knew it.

Know Your Rocks

Sedimentary (sed-ih-MEN-tuh-ree) rocks are created by the buildup of dirt, shells, sand, and other sediment. Over time, this buildup becomes so heavy that the bottom solidifies. Limestone is a type of sedimentary rock. It's built up from layers and layers of seashells. Sandstone is created from layers of sand.

Igneous (IG-nee-us) rocks start deep inside the Earth, where it is so hot that no rock can harden. When a volcano erupts, the molten rock is pushed up onto the surface, where it cools and hardens. Gold and silver are examples of igneous rocks.

Metamorphic (met-uh-MOR-fik) rocks are rocks that have changed from sedimentary or igneous rocks into something different. For example, when limestone is exposed to high temperatures, it is transformed into marble, which is used by artists to create sculptures.

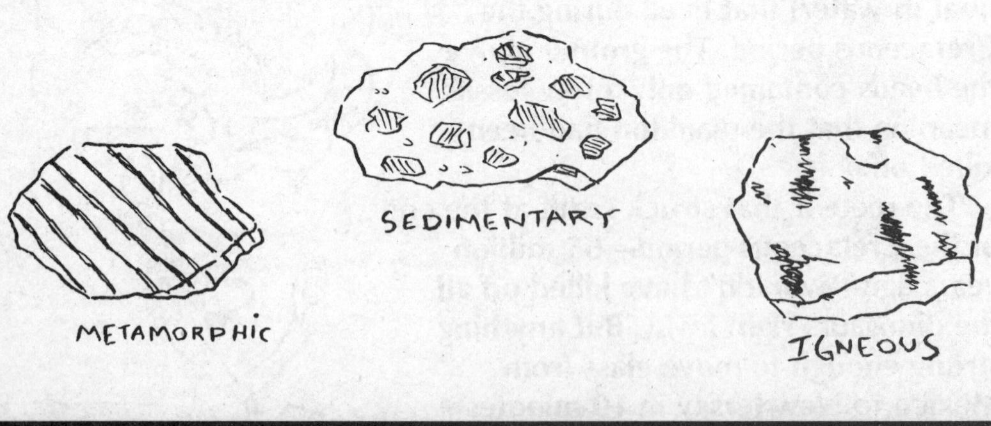

Six-Minute Science
Testing for Limestone

Background:

As you've learned in this chapter, limestone was formed when ancient oceans or lakes dried up, leaving behind seashells, dirt, and rock. Here's a simple test to see if your rocks are made of limestone and were once part of an ancient waterway.

Materials:

- several seashells or eggshells
- drinking glasses or small glass jars
- bottle of lemon juice
- various rocks, pieces of chalk, and pieces of concrete

Procedure:

1. Put the shells inside a small drinking glass.
2. Pour in lemon juice to cover the shells.
3. Note what happens. Limestone is made of seashells. Therefore, any shell with limestone in it should have the same reaction to the lemon juice.
4. Repeat the test with the rocks, chalk, and concrete. Use one sample per glass so you can see which ones are reacting and which are not. Which items contain limestone?

What's Going On?

Seashells and eggshells are made of something called calcium carbonate. The acid in the lemon juice reacts with the calcium carbonate and creates the gas carbon dioxide. You see this reaction in the bubbles fizzing off the shells. Limestone also is made of calcium carbonate. Did any of your rocks show the same reaction as the shells? What about the chalk or the concrete? Are there other substances you'd like to test?

METEOROLOGY

If a butterfly flaps its wings in Beijing [China], it sets people shoveling snow in New York.

USA Today, on how small events have large consequences, 1997

Whenever we want to know if we'll be able to go skiing or swimming on the weekend, we look at the weather forecast. But we often forget it is just that, a forecast—meaning it is a prediction, not a fact. Meteorology is the study of weather, and weather is always changing.

WEATHER OR NOT

Weather is the daily changes in temperature, **precipitation,** air pressure, and the wind's direction and strength. But why does weather change?

Weather starts with the sun. Earth's atmosphere acts like a greenhouse, trapping some of the sun's rays so they stay close to the planet's surface. The heat from those rays is absorbed by water, soil, sand, concrete, plants, houses, and snow. Sand soaks up 75 percent of the rays, and snow absorbs 25 percent. As day becomes night, the heat stored in the ground is released into the air. Light, hot air rises, sometimes carrying **water vapor** with it, while cooler, heavier air falls. This action, called **convection,** is what causes winds and storms.

Global weather patterns are governed by the Earth's orbit and its daily rotation on its axis, both of which create seasons: fall, winter, spring, summer.

Seasons mean certain areas are warmed or cooled for fairly long periods of time. When the Earth moves, so does the atmosphere. Cold air from the northern polar regions collide with warm air from farther south, creating storms.

Weather also is affected by geography. Rochester, New York, is next to Lake Ontario, one of the Great Lakes and also one of the snowiest places in the United States. Clouds pick up water as they float over the lakes, then drop it when they float over land such as Rochester. Mountains, valleys, deserts, oceans, and plains also affect the weather.

In the following experiments, you'll study air pressure and explore the basics of meteorology. Then maybe you can take a stab at predicting the all-too-unpredictable weather.

Experiment

Feeling Some (Air) Pressure?

Background:

You're just about to open a new bottle of soda when your brother sticks a dart through the plastic. How can you keep the soda from running out? Instead of standing around all day with your finger over the hole, get air pressure to work for you.

Materials:

- empty two-liter soda bottle with cap
- hammer and nail

Procedure:

1. Make sure you have permission to use the hammer and nail. You might want to do this experiment outdoors.
2. Fill the soda bottle with water and put the cap on.
3. Stop and think. You are about to make a hole in the bottle. What will happen to the water? Write a hypothesis.
4. Use the hammer and nail to poke a hole in the bottle as shown. Remove the nail.
5. Turn the bottle upside down a few times. What happens? Try dropping the bottle. Did the liquid come out? Now remove the cap. What gives?

What's Going On?

As long as the cap stays on the bottle, you lose very little water through the open hole. But once the cap is off, you've got a fountain. Why? Air pressure.

Air pressure is all around us, squeezing us, pushing us over, and weighing us down, even though we don't feel it happening. Air pressure also is pushing at the soda bottle. When you make a hole in the bottle, gravity tries to pull the water out. But because the cap is on, air pressure pushes the water back in. When the cap is off, air pressure squeezes from the inside of the bottle, pushing the water and helping gravity to pull it out. In the larger world, the amount of air pressure around us is constantly changing, and this in turn causes changes in the weather.

Can you figure out how to get the soda out of the bottle without taking the cap off? Remember, air pressure squeezes the soda from the inside (the operative word here is *squeeze*).

Experiment
Let It Rain

Background:

It rained all day and all night in your neighborhood, but how much rain actually fell? You could listen to the weather report for the answer, but why not measure it yourself? The next time a storm is in the forecast, get your rain gear together.

Materials:

- two or more clear plastic containers (with flat bottoms and parallel sides)
- ruler for each container
- tape
- box to hold the containers

Procedure:

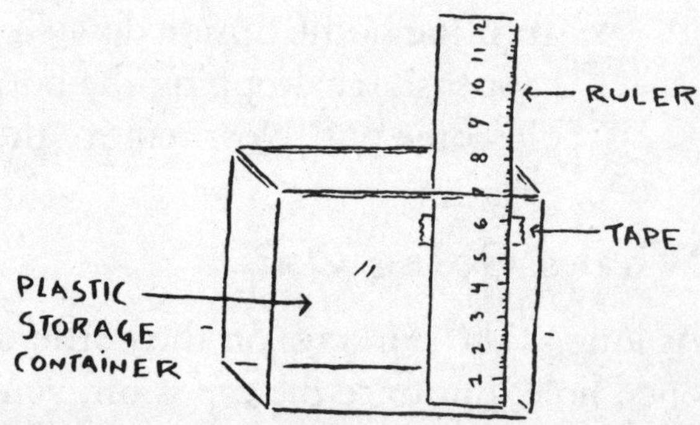

1. Slide a ruler down the inside of each container so it is resting on the bottom as shown. Tape it to the edge of the container. Make sure the ruler is straight up and down, and that the numbers are visible through the side of the container.
2. Place the containers in the box to keep them from being blown over.

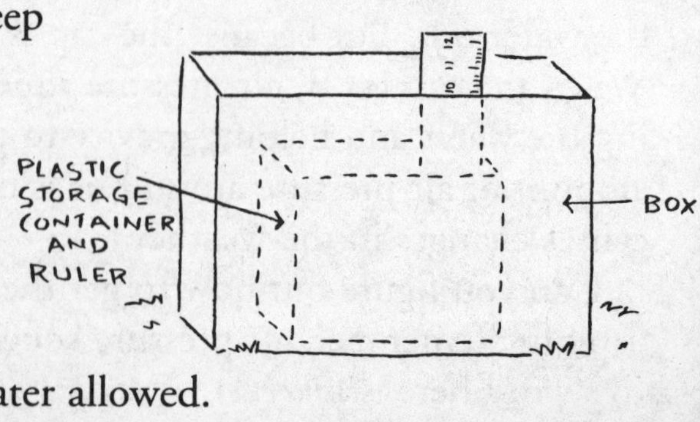

3. Put the box in a secure area outdoors. Do not put it under the edge of a roof. The rain will roll off the roof and into the containers. You want your containers to get an unbiased measurement—no extra water allowed.

4. After it rains and before the sun has had a chance to evaporate the water, record your measurements.
5. As an option, compare your numbers with those from the local weather report. Don't worry if the numbers don't match exactly; weather can change a lot in a small area.
6. Repeat this experiment over the course of several months, keeping track of the precipitation in your notebook.

What's Going On?

When rainfall soaks into the ground, it is impossible to measure how much water came down. By collecting it in a container, you can find out how much actually fell. If you measured one inch of rain, that means a one-inch puddle would be covering your area if the rain didn't run off or seep into the ground.

Want to Do More?

Experiment with different-sized containers. Small containers will give more accurate measurements of small amounts of rain.

KIDSOURCE TIPS

When you look at a rain gauge, you read the measurement as 4. But when your older sister looks at it, she thinks it's almost 5. Who's right? Probably neither of you. You and your sister unknowingly introduced another variable into your experiment: your height. To get an accurate measurement, you need to put your eyes as close to the water level as you can. You'll see that the surface of the water isn't flat, it looks like a bowl. This shape is called a *meniscus* (muh-NIS-kus). Always measure the water level at the *bottom* of the bowl. A water meniscus looks like an upright bowl, but mercury's meniscus looks like an upside-down bowl. How would a milk meniscus be shaped?

REVOLUTIONARY WEATHER

History books tell us that the American Revolution—in which the original 13 American colonies fought to break away from British rule—started because of disagreements over taxes and other issues. But there's another reason you don't hear much about: bad weather.

Before the war began in 1775, harvests were poor, according to climatologist (one who studies weather conditions) William Baron of Northern Arizona State University and historian David Smith of the University of Maine. The farmers and their families weren't starving, but they had little money for luxuries and were angry when the British wanted to tax the New England colonies.

Dr. Baron and Dr. Smith analyzed New England's climate **from about 1700 to 1950. They read farm journals, personal diaries, and local newspapers, and also examined weather-station records from the time. Even though the colonial record keepers had no background in science, their descriptions were very thorough. One entry read: "September 3rd, a severe black frost that laid low all of our vines, corn, and potatoes will make a hungry winter for us." That meant a "killing frost" took place in early fall. Poor crops did not cause the war, but they probably added to the people's overall unhappiness.**

Six-Minute Science
Tea Kettle Cloud

Background:

Clouds are made of water vapor. Steam that comes out of a boiling tea kettle is a type of water vapor. With an adult's supervision, use a tea kettle to make your own cloud, and watch what happens as it cools down.

Materials:

- tea kettle or large pot with lid
- oven mitts (or pot holders)
- cookie sheet

Procedure:

1. Fill the tea kettle or pot about half full with water and put on the stove to boil.
2. When the water has come to a boil, turn off the heat and ask an adult to remove the kettle from the burner.
3. Be careful—the water will be steaming hot and can burn. Put on the oven mitts and open the lid to the tea kettle. Hold the cookie sheet in front of the opening to collect the steam.

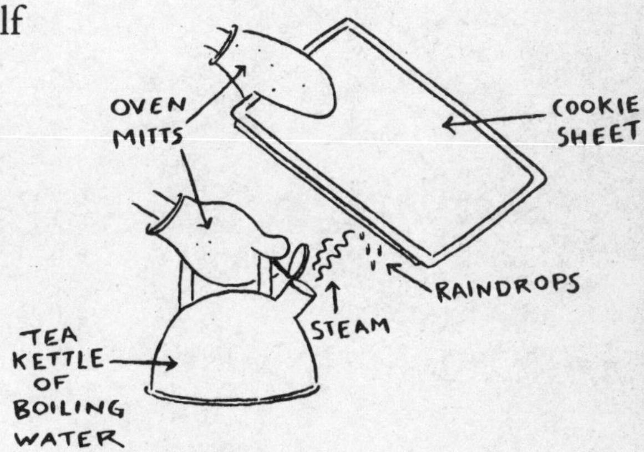

4. Remove the cookie sheet from the steam. Watch what happens as it starts to cool down.

What's Going On?

The cookie sheet is a cool surface compared with the steam from the tea kettle. The steam collects on the sheet, cools, and turns back into water. Eventually, enough water comes together to form drops. In nature, water is evaporated by the sun and turned into vapor. The water vapor rises into the air. When enough vapor collects in the air, clouds form. When those clouds cool down, it rains.

ECOLOGY

Those who dwell as scientists or laymen, among the beauties and mysteries of the Earth, are never alone or weary of life.

Rachel Carson, biologist, 1965

The kind of birdhouse you buy at a store is a wooden box with a small hole in front. If you buy this birdhouse for your favorite bird—say, a bluebird—and you put it in the woods, you won't automatically get a bluebird, because bluebirds don't live in the woods. They live at the edge of fields where they can catch the insects that feed on the tall grass.

As a beginning ecologist, you'll learn the most common areas in which a bluebird lives. You'll also learn that bluebirds need more than a wooden box for a home. They need an entire ***habitat****. The habitat needs them, too. Without bluebirds, there would be more insects. The hungry insects would eat so much of the grass that other animals who also feed on the grass would go hungry.*

GETTING INTO THE HABITAT

Ecology is the study of the relationships that make up habitats, and the connections among plants, animals, rocks, soil, air, and everything else that makes up our planet. Other sciences, including biology, chemistry, geology, meteorology, and physics, play a part in ecology. Ecologists study **ecosystems**. An ecosystem can be an entire desert, or it can be one rotting tree trunk in which insects live. A desert ecosystem is made of sand, small amounts of water, a lot of sunlight, plants such as cacti, and animals such as snakes. Ecologists may study how cactus wrens affect cacti when they use them as homes or hiding places, why plants have waxy skins (the skins help retain moisture), and how the sun helps determine what time of day animals hunt.

Once you understand that the key word is *relationship,* many of the experiments in the other chapters of this book may inspire you to ask ecology-related questions. For example, after doing the "Fruit Fly Farm" experiment on page 23, you may be curious as to how fruit flies interact with their fruit environment (besides eating it, that is). Or, after completing "Black and White" on page 84, you may want to know what effect fur color has on animals that live in warm places and those that live in cold places.

Experiment
What's My Lime?

Background:

Acid rain is created when air pollution combines with water vapor and falls to the ground as rain. This rain can be destructive to lakes, because the pollution makes the water too acidic for plants and animals to survive. The long-term goal is, of course, to stop all pollution. But what can we do in the short term to help clean up our lakes? One solution is to counter the acid with a base.

Before you begin, do the experiment "Are You an Acid?" on page 68.

Materials:

- cabbage leaves
- mixing bowl
- two clear plastic cups or glass jars
- lemon juice
- baking soda

Procedure:

1. (If you have leftover cabbage juice from "Are You an Acid?" go to step 3.) Tear the cabbage leaves into pieces about the size of a quarter. You will need enough to fill one cup.
2. Place the pieces in the bowl. With an adult's help, pour two cups of very hot water over the cabbage. Let sit for 5 minutes. It should turn purple. This will be your cabbage juice.
3. Prepare an experiment chart. You will record the amount of lime (baking soda) you add and the color of the liquid at each step.
4. Pour ½ cup cabbage juice into each plastic cup.
5. Set the first cup aside. The liquid in this cup represents a healthy lake. Your job is to try to match it using the liquid in the second cup.

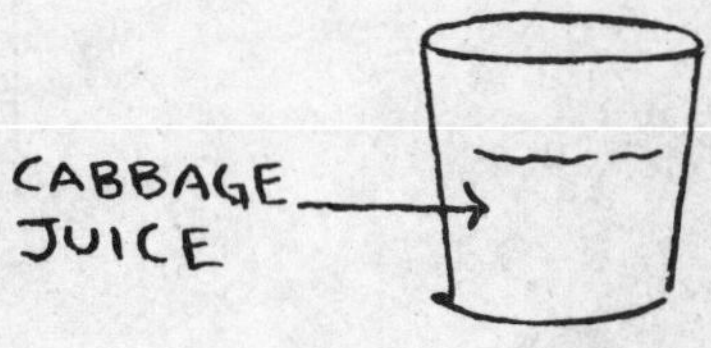

6. Add 4 tablespoons lemon juice to the second cup. The liquid should turn bright red.
7. Over the sink, add ⅛ teaspoon baking soda to the second cup and stir. The mixture will fizz. What color is it?
8. On your chart, record the amount of baking soda added (⅛ teaspoon) and the color of the liquid.

9. Repeat steps 6 through 8 until you come close to matching the color of the "healthy lake." It isn't easy. You may find you need to start over. Try using less baking soda.

What's Going On?

Some things are acidic, and some are basic. Many are in between. Lemon juice is an acid because it turns the cabbage juice red. Baking soda is a base because it turns the juice blue. When a base is added to an acid, the two neutralize each other and the liquid returns to its original color—or close to it.

In many lakes that are affected by acid rain, the acid is too strong to be neutralized by baking soda. Instead, scientists add lime, or calcium oxide, a stronger base. Liming is done in lakes throughout the United States, Canada, and Scandinavia.

Want to Do More?

Test different bases and acids. Try dishwashing detergent, cola, coffee, and tea. Do you get the same results? Can you always change an acid?

Experiment
Ecosystem Field Trip

Background:

What goes into an **ecosystem**? Whenever you're in a natural setting, look around. The longer you observe, the sooner you'll learn to recognize the flora and fauna (that's plants and animals, don'tcha know) that make up an ecosystem.

Materials:

- reference books or field guides on trees, animals, insects, and other forms of nature (available at the library)

Procedure:

1. You'll need to visit three different natural settings. These could include a field, the woods, a large park, and a pond or lake. If any of these areas are far away, ask a parent or other trusted adult to take you there.

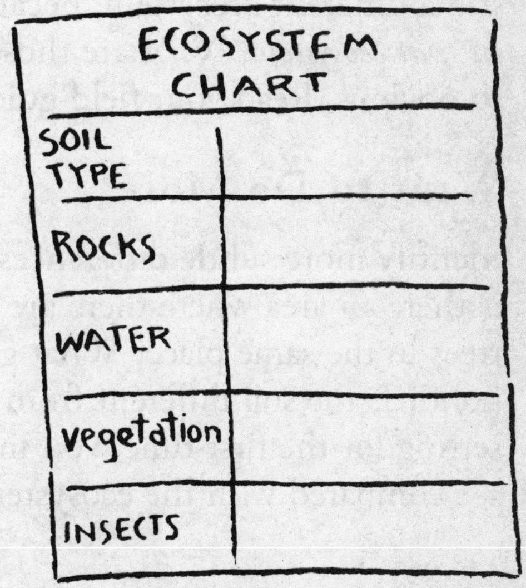

2. Before you leave, make a list of things to observe, such as soil type (sandy, loamy, or clay; see the "Plant Communities" experiment on page 59 for definitions), rocks, water, ground vegetation, bushes, trees, insects, animals, and the amount of sunlight and shade.
3. Go to the first natural setting and find a comfortable place to sit. Go through your list, stopping to look for and observe each item. Use your field guides to identify them. Get up if you need to look more closely at something. What kind of trees and soil do you find? Can you see and identify any animals? If you can't see them, can you hear them?
4. In your notebook, record the time of day and your findings. Sketch some of the plants or animals. Try not to leave until you feel you've gotten to know the area.
5. Visit the other two settings you've chosen and repeat steps 2 through 4.

6. Compare your findings in each setting. What was the same and different in each?

What's Going On?

Every part of an ecosystem has a purpose. Each is like an ingredient in a recipe. If you mix flour, sugar, and yeast, you can make bread. If you mix flour, sugar, and eggs, you can make a cake. You probably found that each setting you visited had some of the same plants and animals—for example, mosquitoes live in the woods, in open fields, and near lakes. But each setting is still a different ecosystem, because each plant or animal serves its own purpose *in that ecosystem*. What are those purposes? Some may be obvious, others not so obvious. Read your field guides and do further research to find out.

Want to Do More?

Identify more subtle differences within an ecosystem. If you are in the woods, is there an area where there are only pine trees? Are there any other kinds of trees in the same place? What grows at the edge of a field, or at the edge of a pond? Is the soil different from one area to the next? When you visit a natural setting for the first time, you may be surprised at how many similarities you see compared with the ecosystems you've already studied.

Experiment
Plant Communities

Background:

Plants can grow in desert sand, in clay, and in loam, which is a mixture of dirt, sand, and clay. But you won't find the same plants in each of these soils. In this experiment, you'll test seedlings to see which soil they prefer.

Materials:

- six small flower pots (the disposable kind that seedlings come in work well)
- old cookie sheet or other tray
- gravel (available at gardening supply stores)
- clay or clay soil (clay soil is reddish or tannish and can be squeezed like clay)
- sand from a sandbox or purchased at a store
- potting soil (available at gardening supply stores)
- seedlings from "How Does Your Garden Grow? (Part 1)" (see page 25), or six store-bought sprouted seeds

Procedure:

1. Arrange the six flower pots on the cookie sheet.
2. Cover the bottom of each pot with gravel.
3. Put the clay or clay soil in two of the pots. Pour sand into the next two. Place potting soil (loam) in the last two. Don't fill them all the way to the top.
4. Place a seedling in each pot. Push each one in gently. The roots should be buried and the stems should stick up.

5. Water the seedlings well and place them in a sunny spot.
6. Write down your hypothesis. For example: "I think the (sand/clay/loam) will be the best soil for this type of plant." Create a chart in your experiment notebook. The first column should be the type of soil. Then make a column for each day of the week.
7. Over the next several weeks, measure the seedlings once a day and record their growth. Add water as needed.
8. When your plants start growing the second set of leaves—their "true leaves"—the experiment is over. Which type of soil was best for this particular plant?

What's Going On?

Seeds start out with enough food stored in their casings to live until they develop roots and true leaves. Your seedlings may have gotten a faster start in sand, but once their stored-up nutrients ran out, they could not find food in the sand. The plants growing in sand probably started to die before the plants in loamy soil did. Clay contains few nutrients as well, and water and air do not move easily through it. Did the seedlings in the clay soil grow? Why or why not? Potting soil is high in nutrients and has good drainage. You should have found that potting soil was the best.

The type of soil in an area determines what kind of plants can grow there. The type of plant determines what kind of insects will come to the area to eat the plant. The type of insect determines what kind of birds will live there to feed on the insects. Soil is, therefore, an important part of every ecosystem.

Want to Do More?

Most plants grow best in loamy soil. But try this experiment with a plant that prefers sand. What happens to a cactus planted in potting soil?

Think of other variables that make up a plant community. What would happen if you put one set of pots in a dark area? What would happen if you watered only one pair of pots? Can you think of a plant that needs little water? In what kind of soil does this plant live?

KIDSOURCE TIPS

Why does the "Plant Communities" experiment use two seedlings for each type of soil instead of just one? Seeds are unpredictable; some will not sprout roots. If you used only four seedlings in this experiment instead of eight, and one of them didn't sprout, you would have to throw out that soil type, or start over. Duplication helps make sure you get accurate results. If you worked with only one seed, and its roots grew upward, how would you know it was unusual? You need at least one other normal-growing seed to show that the wacked-out seed was unique, or not normal.

Experiment
Water Worlds

Background:

Just as it does on land, life underwater varies from place to place. If you were a fish, would you want to live in deep water or shallow water? Where would you go to find seaweed or whatever it is you like to eat? Build an underwater viewer and take a peek into the world below.

Note: Talk about safety issues with your parents or guardians and get their permission and supervision first. Do not go into or near the water by yourself. This may be a good project to do on summer vacation with your family.

Materials:

- empty cardboard quart-size milk container
- scissors
- plastic wrap
- rubber bands

Procedure:

1. Do this experiment on a sunny day. Choose two places—a shallow section and a deep section—at a pond, river, lake, or other water community. Make sure both places have safe access. (If you want to try the ocean, see below under "Want to Do More?")
2. Cut the bottom and top off the milk container.
3. Stretch a piece of plastic wrap over one of the ends. Put a couple of rubber bands over the wrap to hold it tightly in place. This is your underwater viewer.

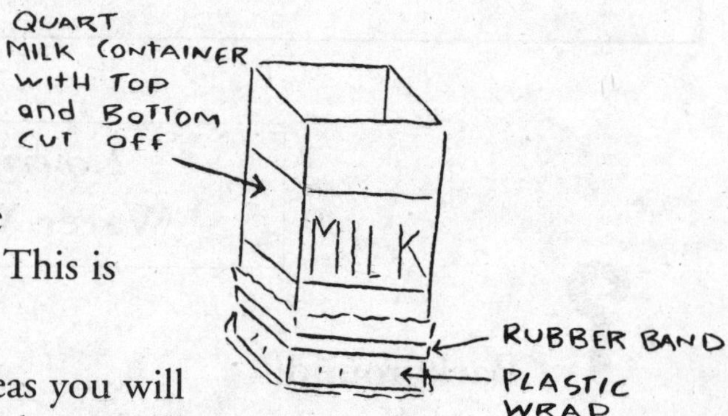

4. Think about the underwater areas you will be exploring. Where do you think you will see more plants and animals? Write out your hypothesis.
5. Take your viewer to the shallow section of the water. Insert it so that the plastic-covered end is submerged in the water. You should be able to see into the water fairly clearly. How do you think the viewer helps?
6. In your experiment notebook, sketch the plants and animals you see. If you see 16 pieces of the same kind of seaweed, draw one piece and write down the number 16 next to it.

7. With a parent or other adult, go to the deep section of the water and repeat steps 5 and 6. Where did you see more animals and plants?

What's Going On?

The viewer works like a swim mask or a pair of goggles, cutting down on surface glare so you can see into the water.

Even underwater, most plants and animals need sunlight and nutrients to survive. You probably found more life in the shallow section, which is closer to the sunlight. Larger fish and animals that do not need as much sunlight may live deep down. Bacteria may live throughout the entire water ecosystem, but you'd need a microscope to see them.

Want to Do More?

Use your viewer to study all sorts of waterscapes. Compare a developed and undeveloped section of a nearby waterway, such as a river where it is bordered by concrete (developed) and where it flows naturally (undeveloped). Development brought on by humans adds dirt that clouds the water. Pollutants also get in, such as garbage, oil, and gasoline washed in from the roads. This cuts down on sunlight and nutrients, causing many plants and animals to die.

You can try this experiment if you're going to the beach, but make sure the ocean water is calm and not too deep. Find an area where the water comes up only waist high. A bay is safer than the open ocean. Again, don't go in the water without an adult. If you get to go on a boat ride, try out your viewer when the boat stops.

Six-Minute Science

The Air Up There

Background:

Is the air in your neighborhood polluted? You can't always see pollution with your eyes. Use this test to check out the air around you.

Materials:

- clean, empty gallon-size milk jug or large tin can
- clean rocks
- white coffee filter or white piece of paper
- magnifying glass

Procedure:

1. If you're using a milk jug, cut it in half (get an adult to help you). If you're using a tin can, make sure the lid is completely off and there are no jagged edges.
2. Put the rocks in the bottom of the container to weigh it down.
3. Line the container with the filter or paper. It's OK if the paper sticks out.
4. Put the container outdoors, uncovered, for a couple of weeks, then bring it back indoors. Carefully remove the paper.
5. Using the magnifying glass, examine the paper. Note any areas that look stained or have dark sediment. These areas could indicate pollution. How would you describe the paper? Is there anything besides pollution that could cause it to change color?
6. Write down your observations in your experiment notebook. Date your entry in case you do this experiment again.

What's Going On?

Exhaust from buses and cars, smoke from factories, and even smoke from fireplaces will discolor the paper and leave *particulate matter*—tiny pieces of soot and other pollutants. Often these pieces are blown away. If they are not, they may become smog—smoke and fog—which floats and casts a brown haze in the air. Natural forces also can discolor the paper. The sun might yellow it, and pollen could leave dust on it. Try to identify these. If necessary, do the experiment again, picking a shady spot away from trees.

Want to Do More?

Is air pollution the same everywhere? Is it the same all year round? If you and your family go on a trip to a place with an environment that's different from where you live, try repeating this experiment. You also could do this project at a different time of year.

Building a Better Stream

In northern Michigan, there's a place with sparkling waterfalls and swift-running streams. But it isn't in some remote forest; it's inside a laboratory. The Stream Research Facility at the University of Michigan's Biological Station is made up of wooden troughs, gutters, and concrete blocks that hold plastic liners through which the water runs. Here, researchers such as Dr. Jan Stevenson of the University of Louisville study how streams work. Dr. Stevenson investigated the effect of sunlight on the growth of algae (AL-jee). Problem algae are the green and brown plant material you see at the edges of lakes and slow-moving waterways. Not only do the algae look bad and cost a lot to clean up, but they also indicate that the water isn't healthy.

The algae weren't always a problem. A long time ago, many streams were lined with shade trees. The problem algae shared the healthy waters with algae called *diatoms* (DY-uh-toms). Diatoms are an important part of the life cycle because they are eaten by insect larvae and snails, which are in turn eaten by fish. Then humans came along and cut down the shade trees. The increase in sunlight caused the problem algae to multiply, crowding out the diatoms and much of the animal and plant life in the water.

By using a greenhouse shade cloth to keep the sun off parts of the laboratory streams, Dr. Stevenson was able to get rid of the problem algae, and the diatoms returned. Because of his work, towns that want to create healthier streams plant shade trees, which allow the diatoms to grow back.

CHEMISTRY

The whole of science is nothing more than a refinement of everyday thinking.

Albert Einstein, physicist, 1936

Take a deep breath. Now let it out. You've just participated in a chemical reaction! First you took air into your lungs. Oxygen from the air went into your bloodstream. Then you exhaled the leftovers.

Chemistry is the study of ***matter*** *and the changes it goes through. Matter is every gas, liquid, and solid in the universe. Chemists examine what makes up matter: the* ***atom****. Atoms are like tiny building blocks. Scientists know of 103 different types of atoms, called the elements. These are organized into a chart known as the Periodic Table of the Elements, which you may have seen in science class or in a laboratory.*

When different types of atoms come together, they form a molecule (MOLL-eh-kyool). A water molecule is made up of two hydrogen atoms (H) and one oxygen atom (O); that's why it is called H_2O*. One drop of water contains 2 million quadrillion molecules of water. That's 2,000,000,000,000,000,000,000 molecules!*

Chemists also need to describe matter itself. Say they were studying milk. They would ask questions about the milk's temperature, its texture, its viscosity (vihs-CAW-sit-ee)—that is, its thickness or thinness—and its color, taste, and smell. Chemists also examine changes the substance might undergo. If lemon juice was added, how would it change the milk? It would cause a chemical reaction that would separate the milk into curds, which can then be made into cheese.

In the experiments that follow, you'll identify acids and bases, make your own crystals, and even play with—ulp—quicksand! As you study matter and its metamorphoses, you will be doing what professional chemists do.

Experiment
Are You an Acid?

Background:

Although you may not know it, chemistry is everywhere you look. Almost all liquids are either acidic or basic (*alkaline* is another word for *basic*). But how do you know which are acids and which are bases? Find out by using your head—a head of red cabbage, that is.

Materials:

- red cabbage (a few large leaves will do)
- large mixing bowl
- five small clear glass jars (baby food jars work well)
- vinegar
- ammonia
- baking soda
- milk
- spoon
- masking tape and pen for labeling

Procedure:

1. Tear the cabbage into shreds about the size of a quarter. You'll need about a cupful.

2. Place the cabbage pieces in the bowl. With help from an adult, pour 4 cups of very hot water over the pieces. Let sit for 5 minutes. It should turn purple. This is your cabbage juice.
3. Write your hypothesis and make a chart for your results. Which samples do you think will be acidic? Which ones will be basic, or alkaline? The first column will contain the name of each sample. Make two more columns, one labeled "Base" and the other "Acid."
4. In each jar, add 4 tablespoons cabbage juice.
5. The first jar will be your control; that is, its contents will maintain the normal color of cabbage juice. You will compare all the other colors to it.
6. Label the second jar "Vinegar" and add 1 teaspoon vinegar. Stir gently with the spoon. Label the next jar "Baking soda" and add 1 teaspoon baking soda. Label the next jar "Ammonia" and add 1 teaspoon ammonia. Label the final jar "Milk" and add 1 teaspoon milk. Stir gently after each addition. What color does the liquid become in each jar? Check off your results in the appropriate column on your chart and write down the color.
7. An acid will turn the juice red. A base will turn the juice blue or green. Put the control jar in the center. Arrange the other jars in order from most basic to most acidic.

What's Going On?

Some things are very acidic, and some are very basic. Many are in between, or neutral. Baking soda and ammonia are bases. Milk and vinegar are acids. Cabbage juice works well for this experiment, but it's not an exact method. That's why chemists created the pH system. In this system, 1 is very acidic, 14 is very basic, and 7 is neutral. Vinegar has a pH of 2.2. Milk is less acidic with a pH of 6.6. Baking soda has a pH of 8.2 and ammonia 12.0. In addition, lemon juice is 2.0, and pure, unpolluted water is 5.6.

Want to Do More?

What other household liquids can you test? Do this experiment with cola and hot tea. If you'd like to try bleach or other cleaning chemicals, get an adult's help. What characteristics does an acid have? How about a base? Look for patterns in the items you test. They are an important part of science.

Save the leftover cabbage leaves or juice for the "What's My Lime?" experiment on page 54.

KIDSOURCE TIPS

There's an unlabeled bottle on the counter. How do you know what's inside? Try smelling it. But be careful—chemicals such as ammonia are dangerous if inhaled too deeply. And we don't mean putting your nose right up to the bottle. Read on.

Ammonia, vinegar, and dishwashing soap each have a unique scent. For safety's sake, it's important that you learn to recognize these if you're going to be working with chemicals. Take the cap off the mystery bottle and then stand at least a foot away. Use your hands to wave some of the vapor from the open bottle toward you. Gently inhale for just a second. If you smell something strong that you think may be dangerous, back away and notify a parent.

Experiment
Cultivating Crystals

Background:

There are two types of solids, amorphous (uh-MOR-fus) and crystalline (KRIS-tuh-lihn). Most solids are amorphous—that is, the atoms are put together in no particular order. In crystals, however, the atoms are in a pattern, and this pattern is repeated as the crystal gets larger. In this experiment, you'll create a crystal garden. Be patient; this takes a week or more, depending on how dry and hot your home is.

Materials:

- two clean, clear glass jars without lids (mayonnaise jars work well)
- several lengths of clean string
- two pencils
- tape
- scissors
- clean paper clips
- soup bowl
- sugar
- salt
- spoon
- masking tape and pen for labeling

Procedure:

1. Set up the jars on a tabletop.
2. Tie one or more pieces of string to each pencil and tape them in place so they won't slip. The string should reach the bottom of the jar, with a little extra. Trim the string as needed.

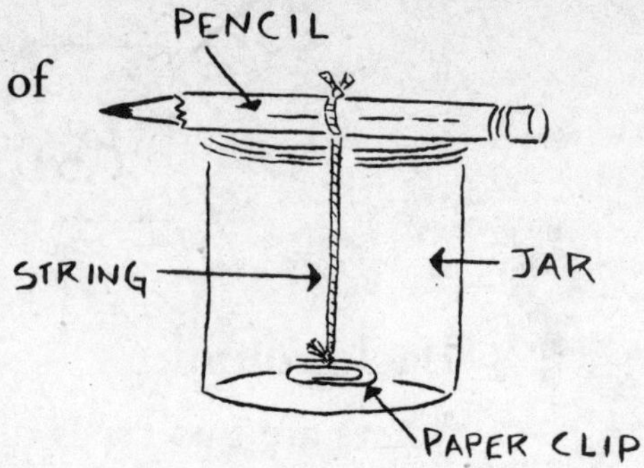

3. Tie a paper clip to the end of each piece of string to weigh it down. The paper clip should lie flat on the bottom of the jar. Take the string and paper clip out of the jar.

4. To start your crystal garden, pour ½ cup hot water into the soup bowl.

5. Add 1 cup sugar, then 2 tablespoons sugar. Stir until dissolved. The mixture will be thick and syrupy, but somewhat clear.

6. Carefully pour the mixture into the first jar. Lay a pencil across the mouth of the jar and drop the string inside. Label this jar "Sugar" and set it in a warm, dry place (a south-facing window works well).

7. Rinse out the bowl and pour ½ cup hot water into it. Add 3 tablespoons salt. Stir until dissolved.

8. Pour the mixture into the second jar. Lay the other pencil on top of the jar and drop the string inside. Label this jar "Salt" and set it next to the first jar.

9. Check the jars daily. As the liquid evaporates, crystals will form on the string. Draw the shapes of the crystals in your experiment notebook.

What's Going On?

As the water evaporates, it forces the sugar and salt to move closer and closer until they form crystals, which build on one another like bricks. Crystals are pure; there is nothing "extra" in them. When chemists get crystals, they know they have a pure sample.

You started this experiment with a saturated solution—one that has been filled until it can hold no more. Only a little water had to evaporate in order to push the sugar and salt molecules closer together. Because your crystal garden is made of plain sugar or salt and water, you can eat it! But remember: Never eat an experiment when you don't know exactly what is in it, or if it involves anything that isn't food.

Want to Do More?

To ½ cup hot water, add 2 tablespoons Epsom salts (sold at drugstores). Instead of using string, pour the mixture into a shallow dish. Crystals will form along the liquid's edge as the water evaporates.

Experiment

Instant Quicksand!

Background:

Is this quicksand look-alike a solid? Is it a liquid? Play with it, but make sure you don't get stuck in the muck!

Materials:

- newspaper
- cornstarch
- mixing bowl
- food coloring (optional)
- spoon

Procedure:

1. Spread newspaper over your work area. This experiment can get messy.
2. Place ⅔ cup cornstarch in the mixing bowl.
3. Mix in ⅓ cup water. (You may have to use your fingers to break up the cornstarch lumps.) Add food coloring if desired.
4. Add a little more water to the cornstarch mixture and stir with the spoon. Continue adding water and stirring until the mixture is the texture of wet sand. Keep stirring even though it gets difficult. Get help if you need it. (If the mixture turns to liquid, add more cornstarch.)

5. Once you've got your "quicksand," play with it. Jab it hard with your finger. Then insert your finger into it slowly. Can you describe the difference? Pinch off a piece and roll it between your fingers. What does it feel like? What does it smell like? Try to roll it into a ball. What happens? Throw a gob of it on some newspaper. What do you observe?

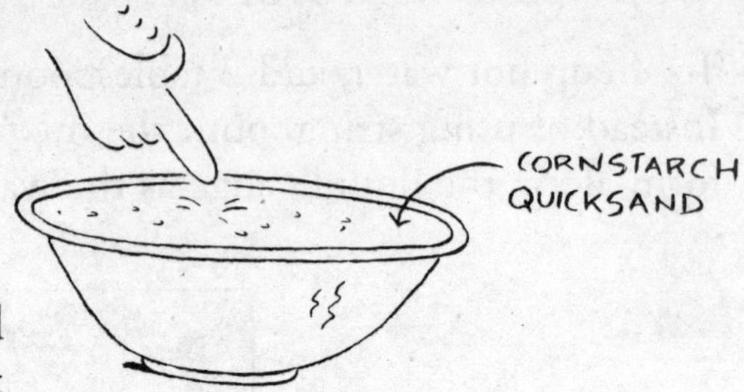

6. Write your observations in your experiment notebook.

What's Going On?

Have you ever seen one of those old movies where someone gets caught in quicksand? This cornstarch mixture is similar. It behaves differently depending on how you treat it. Little particles of cornstarch are suspended in the water, which makes the mixture a *colloid* (KALL-oyd). Skim milk is a colloid because it is a suspension of solids (mostly proteins) in water. Pudding is a suspension of starch and water, like your cornstarch quicksand.

Want to Do More?

Make your quicksand again, but this time add even more water in steps (keep track of how much water you use so you can make it again if you want). What happens to the mixture? Make a series of these mixtures using different amounts of water. How would you describe each?

KIDSOURCE TIPS

Don't throw your instant quicksand down the sink. It could harden and block the plumbing. Instead, add water until the mixture becomes completely liquid. Or, toss the quicksand into the trash.

WHAT A GAS

How can you measure something you can't see? By using a laser.

In a research plane, scientists trap air (gas) inside chambers and shoot a laser through it. Nitrogen dioxide (NO_2), a toxic gas, in the air absorbs the laser beam and gives off a light. The scientists use that to measure how much NO_2 is in the atmosphere. To detect different gases or chemicals, researchers use lasers that produce different-colored lights.

Dr. Bill Brune of Pennsylvania State University is using a similar technique to study smog in Nashville, Tennessee. He and his team are focused on a molecule called hydroxyl (hy-DROKS-ul), or OH, which is made up of oxygen (O) and hydrogen (H). Dr. Brune shines lasers through the air. The OH molecules in the air absorb the laser's energy and give off a glow. The researchers measure the glow to find out how much hydroxyl is in the air.

OH is involved in almost every type of air pollution known. When exhaust is expelled from cars and smokestacks, hydroxyl breaks down these gases, called hydrocarbons, into smaller pieces. These pieces are carried up into the air by water vapor and eventually rain back down to Earth. If OH did not break down the hydrocarbons, they would build up to dangerous levels. That's why hydroxyl is called "the detergent of the atmosphere."

Six-Minute Science

More Balloon Magic

Background:

You don't see it, but gas takes up space all around us. By creating a chemical reaction to make carbon dioxide, you can see just how much space it needs.

Materials:

- funnel
- baking soda
- empty plastic soda bottle
- vinegar
- balloon that fits over the mouth of the soda bottle

Procedure:

1. Do this experiment over a sink or a dishpan. It can get messy.
2. Using the funnel, pour 1 tablespoon baking soda into the soda bottle. Tap the sides of the funnel to get all the baking soda in. Rinse out the funnel.
3. Use the funnel to pour ½ cup vinegar into the balloon. Pinch the neck of the balloon so that all of the vinegar is trapped inside.

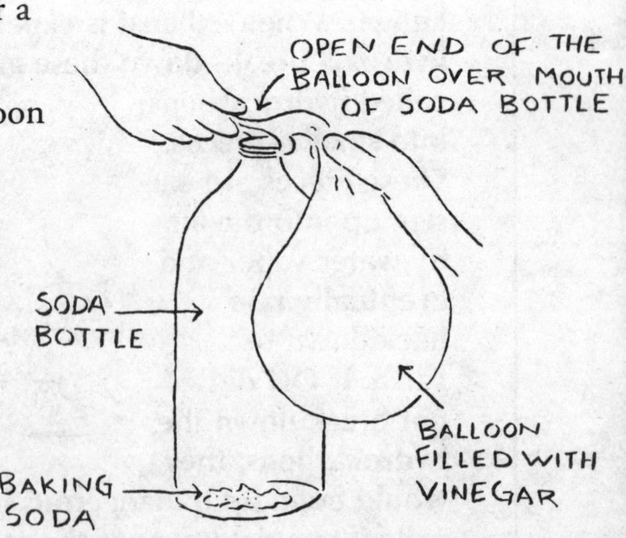

4. Keeping the vinegar in the balloon, carefully roll the opening of the balloon over the mouth of the soda bottle.

5. Hold the balloon and bottle in one hand. With your other hand, lift the balloon upright so all of the vinegar pours into the bottle as shown.

6. Can you feel the chemical reaction as you hold the bottle? What happens to the balloon?

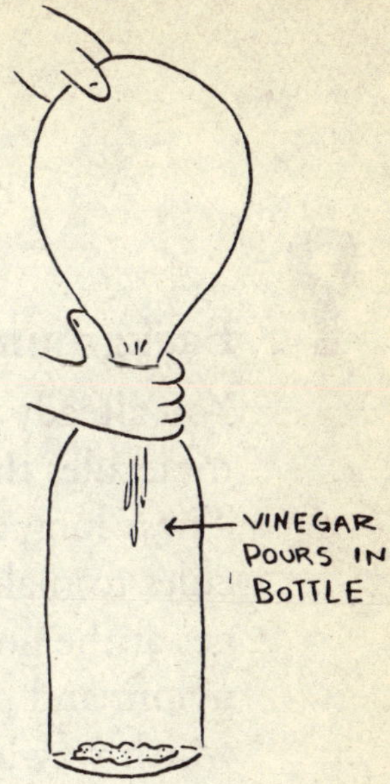

What's Going On?

When baking soda mixes with vinegar, the combination creates carbon dioxide. This gas needs space, so it tries to escape, pushing the liquid up and out of the bottle. As the liquid rises, it takes some of the gas bubbles and creates foam, a mixture of liquid and gas. Meanwhile, the gas that gets through blows up the balloon.

Want to Do More?

Try using a regular drinking glass, some salt, and carbonated soda. Add a pinch of salt to the soda and watch what happens. This time, the salt needs space, so it's the bubbles that are being pushed out of the way.

Six-Minute Science
Exploring Polymers

Background:

You already know molecules are collections of atoms. Polymers are molecules that are hooked together like a chain of paper clips. These long chains are woven together with short groups of molecules to make a strong and flexible material. The plastic bags you get at the grocery store are made of a polymer, and so are rubber, nylon, and parts of wood. This experiment will help you learn which way long chains of molecules are oriented.

Materials:

- newspaper
- plastic bag
- scissors

Procedure:

1. Spread out a section of newspaper as if you were going to read it. Grasp the top with both hands and make a tear partway down the page. How does the rip move? Is it straight or jagged?
2. Turn the paper 90 degrees so that the words are running vertically. Grasp the top and tear again. You are starting at a different edge this time. What happens?
3. Do the same with a plastic bag. You may need to start the tear by cutting a slit in the bag.

What's Going On?

Newspaper is made of a polymer called cellulose (SELL-yoo-lohs), and plastic bags are made of polypropylene (paw-lee-PROH-puh-leen). Most are constructed so that the long chains of polymers are running perpendicular (at a right angle). If this is the case with the newspaper and bag you used, then the first tear should have created a straight rip because you were tearing *along* the chains of polymers. When you get a jagged rip, you are tearing *across* the chains, which makes it hard to tear straight.

CHAPTER 8

PHYSICS

A scientist in his laboratory is not only a technician; he is also a child placed before natural phenomena which impress him like a fairy tale.

Marie Curie, chemist

OK, drop everything! Well, just drop this book. What happens? It falls to the ground. Put a different way, gravity pulls the book toward the Earth.

Physics is the study of how energy and matter interact. You knew what would happen before you let go of the book. In fact, you may have been so sure that you didn't even drop the book. You have reason to be certain. You've been exploring the effects of gravity since you were a baby. In all that time, gravity has never allowed anything to fall upward.

Gravity may be obvious, but other forces in our world are not. Sir Isaac Newton is best known for discovering gravity, but he also studied how objects move. He learned that an object tends to move in a straight line, and that when an object is at rest, it remains so unless it is acted on by an outside force. Just about everything in our universe follows this rule. It's called Newton's First Law of Motion, and it describes a force called ***inertia*** *(in-ER-shuh). If you threw a stone into outer space, it would keep going and going. If you threw that stone on Earth, inertia tries to keep the stone moving in a straight line, but there are other forces, such as gravity, that pull it down.*

Physicists look at the big picture (such as stars and black holes), and the ultratiny picture (atoms and parts of atoms, for instance). Once they understand how energy and matter interact on Earth, they can find out how it interacts on Mars, Venus, Pluto, and the rest of the galaxy.

In the following experiments, you'll investigate the mechanics of physics and examine the basic forces that govern our world. As you'll learn, physics is everywhere.

Experiment
Friction Function

Background:

If you toss a marble up in the air, you know gravity will pull it down. But if you roll a marble across the carpet, what makes it stop? The answer is friction. **Friction** is a force that resists motion between two solid objects: the marble and the carpet. In this experiment, you'll determine which of three surfaces will have the most and least friction.

Materials:

- sheet of stiff cardboard, approximately 3 feet long and at least 6 inches wide
- books
- solid wooden block, such as a child's toy
- stopwatch or watch with a second hand
- aluminum foil
- sandpaper
- tape

Procedure:

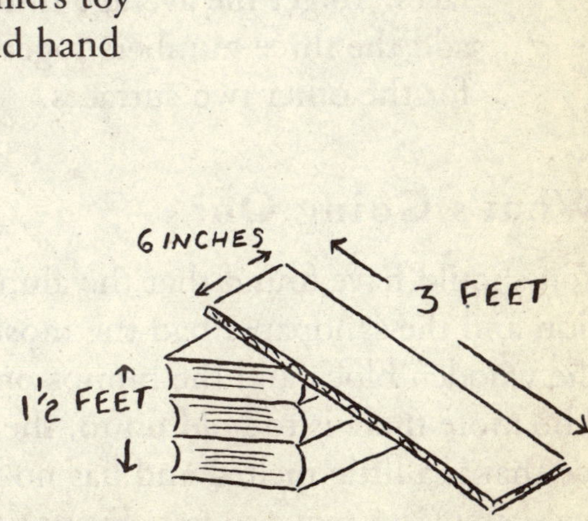

1. Build a ramp by propping up the cardboard with the books. At the high end, your ramp should be about half as tall as it is long. For example, a 3-foot-long ramp should be 1½ feet tall.

2. Create a table in your experiment notebook. You will need five columns and three rows. Label the first column "Surfaces" and list the three surfaces your block will be touching: cardboard, aluminum foil, and sandpaper. Label the next three columns "Time Trial 1," "Time Trial 2," and "Time Trial 3." Label the last column "Time Trials Average."
3. Write out your hypothesis. Which surface do you think will provide the fastest descent? Which will provide the slowest?
4. Let the block roll down the ramp, timing its descent with the stopwatch. Record how much time it took on your chart. Send the block down two more times and record the results.
5. Wrap aluminum foil around the ramp, keeping the surface as smooth as possible.
6. Repeat step 4 with the aluminum-wrapped ramp. Take off the foil.
7. Tape sandpaper to the ramp, rough side up. It does not need to cover the entire width of the cardboard, but it should cover the entire length. You may need to tape a few pieces together.
8. Repeat step 4 with the sandpaper-covered ramp.
9. Next, figure out the average descent time for each of the three surfaces. To get the average time for the cardboard surface, for example, add the three numbers together and divide by three. Now do the same for the other two surfaces.

What's Going On?

You should have found that the aluminum foil had the least amount of friction and the sandpaper had the most. Friction occurs because the bumps on the wooden block and the bumps on the sandpaper grab on to each other. The more there is to hold on to, the more friction there is. Ice is slippery, but ice that is a little melted and has no bumps is even more slippery. This is why ice skaters can move so fast. Every time a skater puts a foot forward, the pressure of the blade melts the ice a little. That water lubricates the rest of the blade, and the skater can glide with very little friction.

Want to Do More?

Test out other surfaces. What happens if you put wax paper on the ramp, or notebook paper? Go outdoors and try putting water or cooking oil on the ramp. What do you think will happen?

KIDSOURCE TIPS

Why do you need to take an average of the three time trials in the above experiment? Averages smooth out data so that you get a good representation of what happened. Say you had a wooden block that went down the cardboard ramp in 4 seconds, then 10 seconds, then 7 seconds. You need only one number, so you figure out the average, which is 7 (4 + 10 + 7 = 21; 21 ÷ 3 = 7). Then you sent the block down the foil-covered ramp and got 4 seconds each time. Your average would be 4. However, if you weren't using averages, you might think the cardboard and the foil results were the same, because you got 4 in the first trial with the cardboard.

Experiment
Black and White

Background:

The sun warms our planet, but not every area heats up at the same rate. Which do you think will get hotter faster, a tin can covered in black, or one covered in white? Which one will cool down faster? Break out the thermometers! It's time to learn how color affects temperature.

Materials:

- two clean, empty soup cans
- electrical tape or duct tape
- one white sheet and one black sheet of construction paper
- scissors
- cellophane or transparent tape
- two thermometers
- desk lamp (optional)

Procedure:

1. Carefully cover any rough edges on the cans with electrical or duct tape. Get help from an adult for this.
2. Cut the white construction paper so it fits all the way around the first can. Wrap the can in the paper and tape it in place with regular tape. Fold the edges inside and underneath the can.
3. Repeat step 2 with the black construction paper and the second can.
4. Fill the cans ¾ full with room-temperature water. Place a thermometer in each.

5. Which can will heat up faster and which will cool down faster? Write two hypotheses.
6. Create two charts in your experiment notebook, one for the white can and one for the black can. Each chart has two columns, one labeled "Time" and the other "Temperature."
7. Put the cans side by side in a sunny spot, such as a south-facing window. Or, place them under a bright desk lamp. The lamp should be about 12 inches from the cans.
8. Record the starting time and temperatures on your chart.
9. Every 15 minutes, record the thermometers' readings.
10. After an hour, move the cans to a cool, dark spot. If you are using a lamp, turn it off and move it away from the cans.
11. Record the temperatures every 15 minutes for another hour.
12. Create two graphs in your notebook. The X axis is time, the Y axis is temperature (see the section called "Graphs" in chapter 2). Connect the dots on the graphs. Which can heated up faster? Which cooled down faster?

What's Going On?

Colors absorb and release heat at different rates. Black absorbs light and turns it into heat. White acts as a reflector, bouncing most of the light energy (and potential heat) off. What happened when the cans were moved away from the light? The color that absorbs the heat faster also radiates, or releases, it faster. You should have found that the black can gets hotter faster, but it also cools down faster.

Want to Do More?

What do you think will happen if you cover a can with navy blue paper, or light pink paper? Try this experiment using the whole spectrum of colors.

Experiment
Parachuting In

Background:

Have you ever dreamed about skydiving? This experiment will help you live out your fantasy. You'll make two parachutes, a big one and a small one. Which one do you think will have a longer "hang time"?

Materials:

- plastic garbage bag
- scissors
- eight pieces lightweight string, each about 20 inches long
- two pieces lightweight string, each about 3 inches long
- two small metal washers
- stopwatch or watch with a second hand

Procedure:

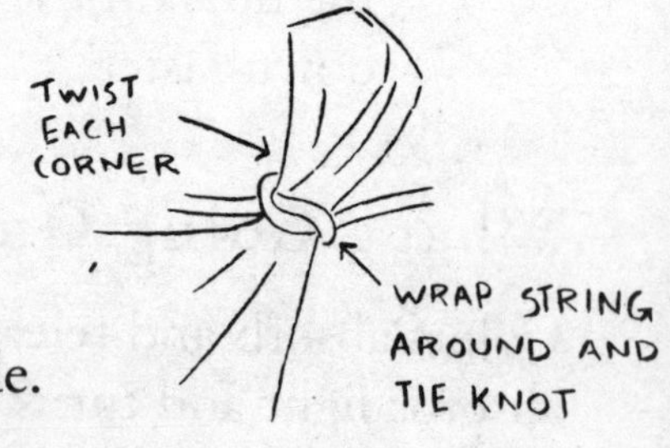

1. You'll need a friend's help for this experiment. To make the first parachute, cut a square from the plastic bag. It should be 24 inches on each side.
2. Twist one corner as shown. Wrap the end of one of the 20-inch pieces of string around the twist. Tie a square knot.

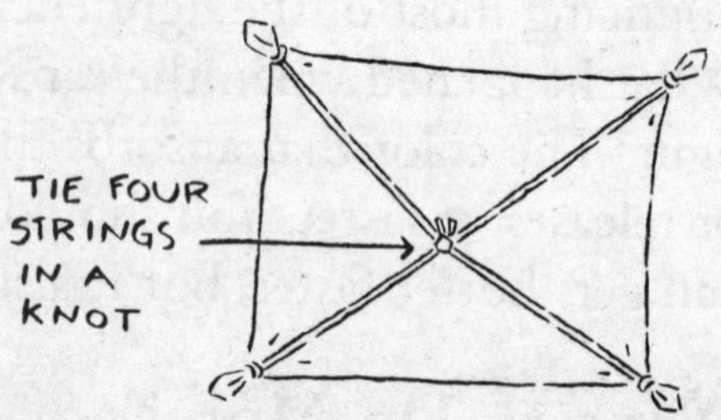

3. Repeat step 2 for the other three corners of the square.
4. Gather the strings in the center of the square. Tie the ends of all four strings together in one overhand knot as shown.

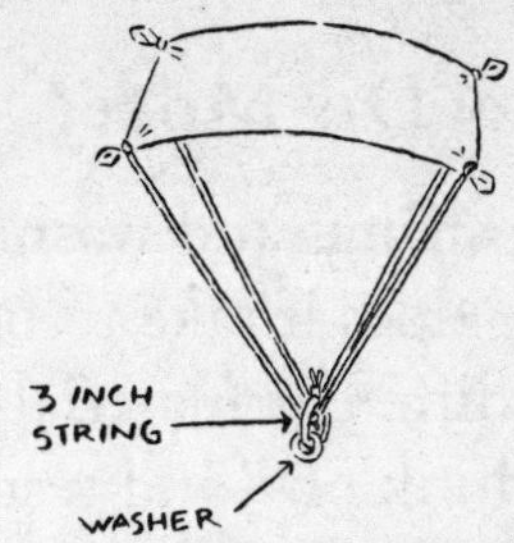

5. Slip a short piece of string through a washer. Use a square knot to tie the string and washer to the four long strings as shown.

6. Pull up the center of the square so that the parachute collapses like a closed umbrella as shown. Put the parachute aside.

7. For the second parachute, cut another square from the plastic bag that is 12 inches on each side. Repeat steps 2 through 6.

8. Prepare a chart in your experiment notebook to record the time it takes for the parachutes to fall. Make two columns, one labeled "Parachute" and the other labeled "Time." Then create two rows, one for each parachute.

9. Which parachute do you think will take longer to land on the ground? Write out your hypothesis.

10. Go to a second-story window or to the top of a stairwell. Have your friend stand on the ground below with the stopwatch. Hold the first parachute so that the washer is hanging down. Drop it out the window or down the stairwell. DO NOT LEAN OUT THE WINDOW. The parachute should open.

11. Record the time it takes for the parachute to land. Repeat for the second parachute. You may want to do several tests for each parachute and average the results.

What's Going On?

The large parachute should have floated slowly to the ground. The smaller parachute should have come down more quickly. Why? Air is pushing upward on the parachute even though gravity is pulling it down. The large parachute has more air resistance, the same thing that causes a feather to float to the ground. The more area a parachute has, the more air will push on it, keeping it up.

Want to Do More?

Wrap the strings and washer around the parachute and throw it up in the air. How long does it take to unwrap and open up? Try making parachutes out of scraps of different material—cotton, wool, nylon, foil, paper, or anything else you can think of—and test which works best.

TO CATCH A NEUTRINO

All matter, everything around you—solid, liquid, or gas—is made up of tiny, constantly moving particles called atoms. Within each atom are billions of even tinier particles. The three biggest are neutrons, protons, **and** electrons. **Neutrons and protons make up the *nucleus,* or core, of the atom. Electrons orbit the nucleus.**

***Neutrinos* (noo-TREE-nohz) fill the space between the electrons and the nucleus. In the time it took you to read this, more than one million billion of these particles have passed through your body! Neutrinos are created when other particles decay. By studying them, we can learn more about supernovas (exploding stars), black holes (stars that have collapsed), and quasars (bright, starlike objects).**

That's why physicists built a neutrino trap. They put it in the Antarctic, where the ice is crystal clear. Boiling water was poured on the ice sheet and holes were dug more than a mile deep to lay the trap. The trap is a telescope named AMANDA (Antarctic Muon and Neutrino Detector Array). Most telescopes look up, but not AMANDA. It looks deep down into the ice. When a neutrino runs into a nucleus, it lets off another particle called a *muon* (MYOO-on). The muon then gives off a blue light. By analyzing this light with AMANDA, researchers can tell where the neutrino came from and whether the stars near the neutrino's home went supernova.

Six-Minute Science
Racing with Gravity

Background:

How fast can your body react to stop gravity? Find out by using nothing more than a 12-inch ruler. Oh, and a friend, too.

Material:

- ruler

Procedure:

1. Stand next to your friend. Hold out your hands as if you were going to clap. Your friend should hold the ruler vertically, with the number "1" on the bottom. Have him hold the ruler above the space between your outstretched hands.
2. When your friend lets go of the ruler, try to catch it before it lands on the ground. If you are successful, look at the number on the ruler where you caught it.
3. Let your friend give it a try. Compare your findings.

What's Going On?

Gravity pulls everything down at a constant rate. You are competing with gravity to see if your body can react fast enough to catch the ruler before it falls more than 12 inches.

CHAPTER 9

ELECTROMAGNETICS

Research is formalized curiosity. It is poking and prying with a purpose.

Zora Neale Hurston, writer

More than once, you've probably dragged your sock-covered feet across a carpet and shocked a friend by touching her arm. Or, you may have been on the receiving end of the zap. You were having fun—or maybe not, depending on your point of view—with static electricity. But did you know you can block that shock next time by using an ***insulator****?*

Electromagnetics is a branch of physics, and it's all about charge. Charge is what you picked up from that carpet. The charge moves through your body and is released when you make contact with someone else. Your body serves as the ***conductor****. As you learned in chapter 8, atoms are made up of electrons, neutrons, and protons. Electrical charges come from electrons and protons.*

Unlike charges attract, and like charges ***repel****. A negatively charged electron will come together with a positively charged proton, but two electrons will move away from each other. When an electron is "rubbed off," the atom becomes charged and is now called an ion. The loose electron and the ion move around frantically, trying to reconnect with other atoms. This is what creates electricity.*

You can feel these charges when you play with static electricity. Blow up a balloon and rub it on your hair. You have just rubbed electrons off your hair and onto the balloon. Now touch the balloon to some scraps of paper. The paper should stick to the balloon. The positive charges in the paper were attracted to the negative charges on the balloon, causing them to stick together.

An electric current results when electrons float around a ***circuit****. The electrons move through a conductor—usually a metal wire—from the negatively charged part of a battery to the positively charged one. As you'll learn in the experiments that follow, some materials make better conductors than others. Materials that don't let electrons move at all are called insulators.*

As you experiment with electromagnetics in this chapter, you'll feel a force of nature right under your fingertips.

Experiment
The Everlasting Static Electricity Machine

Background:

It's fun to run your feet along the carpet and shock a friend. But to generate another spark, you have to drag your feet on the carpet again. There is a way to make the spark last. Build this device, invented by Alessandro Volta in 1775. Why doesn't the charge disperse after every zap of static electricity?

Materials:

- paper or Styrofoam cup
- aluminum pie plate
- tape or glue
- piece of wool
- plastic plate or tray big enough to hold the pie plate
- fluorescent lightbulb (optional)

Procedure:

1. This experiment does not work well on hot and humid days. Wait until it's cool and dry.

2. Tape or glue the cup to the center of the pie plate. This will be the "handle" for the plate.
3. The plastic plate will be your base. Rub the piece of wool on the plastic.
4. Holding it by the handle, place the pie plate on the plastic base. What happens?
5. Now touch the plastic base with one finger. What happens?
6. Lift the pie plate off the base by the handle.
7. Hold your knuckle near the pie plate. Did you draw any sparks? They might sting a little. Try holding a fluorescent lightbulb to the plate. What happens?
8. Repeat steps 4 through 7. Do you have to rub the base with the wool again?

What's Going On?

When you rubbed the base with the wool, you charged the plastic. Loose electrons jumped from the plastic onto the wool, leaving the plastic with a positive charge (remember, electrons are negatively charged, protons are positively charged). When you put the pie plate on the base, nothing happened. The electrons didn't move immediately from the base to the plate. They needed a conductor: your finger.

When you touched your finger to the base, the negative electrons in your body were attracted to the positive charge in the plastic. Now the pie plate is negatively charged, and the base is positively charged. When you lift up the pie plate, you are tearing apart these charges and creating a spark. The pie plate doesn't run out of sparking power because your body serves as an electrical ground. The charge on the plate comes from you, and your body has an almost infinite amount of positive and negative charges.

Want to Do More?

Take your Everlasting Static Electricity Machine and get a straw, a string, some tape, and a ball of aluminum foil. Tape the ball to one end of the string. Tape the straw flat on the top of the cup. Now tape the string and ball to the straw so that the ball almost touches the aluminum pie plate. Repeat the experiment above and watch what happens to the foil ball.

Experiment

Conductors vs. Insulators

Background:

Conductors are materials that allow electrons to flow from one place to another. This is the basis of electricity. Copper wire is a good conductor. What other household items are good conductors? Build an electrical circuit and find out.

Materials:

- electrical wire (use single conductor wire, sold at hardware stores)
- pocketknife or scissors
- clothespin
- flashlight bulb (2-volt or 1.5-volt; a 3-volt bulb may not work)
- size D battery
- materials to test: a penny, a paper clip, a stone, a rubber band, paper

Procedure:

1. You are going to test several materials to see if they are good conductors. Write down your predictions in your experiment notebook.
2. With an adult's help, cut 10 inches of wire. Peel away some of the plastic covering on the ends of the wires to expose the metal.

3. Open the clothespin and insert the base of the flashlight bulb into the rounded section.

4. Touch the exposed metal end of the wire to the side of the bulb's metal base. Use the clothespin to hold it in place.

5. Now test your circuit. You'll need a friend to help you do this. Hold the metal tip on the end of the lightbulb to the end of the size D battery. Touch the other end of the wire to the other end of the battery as shown. The bulb should light up. If it doesn't, make sure enough exposed wire is touching the base of the bulb. If your circuit still does not work, you may have a defective lightbulb or battery.

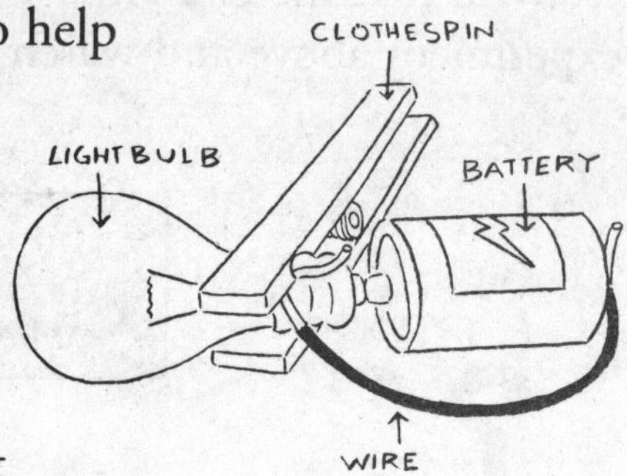

6. Test your materials by putting them between the battery and the wire. Have your friend hold the lightbulb's metal tip to one end of the battery. Hold the penny on the other end of the battery, then touch the wire to the side of the penny that is facing away from the battery. What happens to the bulb?

7. Repeat step 6 for the remaining materials. Trade places with your friend so each of you gets to handle both ends of the circuit.

8. Record the outcome of each test in your experiment notebook.

What's Going On?

Electrons flow through some materials but are blocked by others. When they flow through, that material is a conductor. When they are blocked, that material is an insulator.

Experiment
Building a Galvanometer

Background:

A *galvanometer* (gal-vuh-NAW-met-er) measures the presence, direction, and strength of an electric current. The galvanometer in this experiment also will show how electricity affects magnetic fields. Remember that a compass always points toward magnetic north unless there is some kind of interference. You are going to create this interference.

Materials:

- electrical wire, about 12 inches long
- compass
- size D battery
- tape

Procedure:

1. Starting about 2 inches from one end, wrap the wire around the compass three times. Make sure you can see the compass needle through the wire.
2. Tape the long end of the wire to the end of the size D battery. The wire's exposed metal part should be touching the battery's metal base. If the wire is not exposed, peel back some of the covering.
3. What do you think will happen to the compass needle when electricity is sent through the wire? Write a hypothesis in your experiment notebook. Be sure to record what direction the needle is pointing toward before you proceed.

4. Touch the short end of the wire to the other end of the battery. What happens to the needle?

What's Going On?

The needle jumped! When an electrical current passes through a conductor, in this case the wire, the magnetic needle turns at a right angle to the conductor. How much the needle turns indicates the strength of the current.

Want to Do More?

What happens if you repeat this experiment using a stronger battery? What happens if you wrap more wire around the compass?

Six-Minute Science

Bending over Backward

Background:

You've seen static electricity make paper stick to a balloon. But did you know that even water is attracted to electricity? It will bend and twist, trying to connect.

Materials:

- balloon
- stream of running water (use a deep sink, a bathtub, or a garden hose)
- tissue paper

Procedure:

1. Do this experiment on a cool, dry day. Blow up the balloon and tie a knot to keep the air in.

2. Rub the balloon on your hair to charge it up.
3. Hold the balloon next to the stream of water and watch the water try to connect.
4. Repeat the experiment using tissue paper instead of water.

What's Going On?

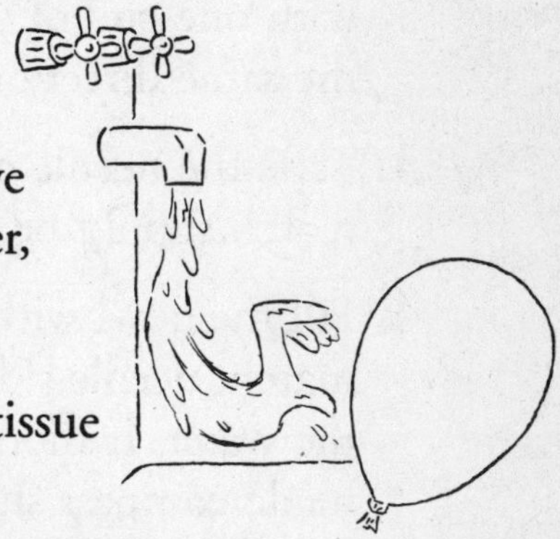

When you rubbed the balloon on your hair, you transferred electrons to the balloon, leaving it with a negative charge. Then, when you held the balloon near the water, the water quickly rearranged its positive and negative charges so that the positive charges were closer to the balloon's negative charges. The same thing happens to tissue paper when it is brought close to the balloon.

Six-Minute Science
Showing a Little Compass-ion

Background:

You can make a compass using a magnet and a simple sewing needle. You won't be able to carry it around, but like store-bought compasses, this one will always point north.

Materials:

- bar magnet
- sewing needle
- flat paper matchstick
- tape
- glass or plastic bowl

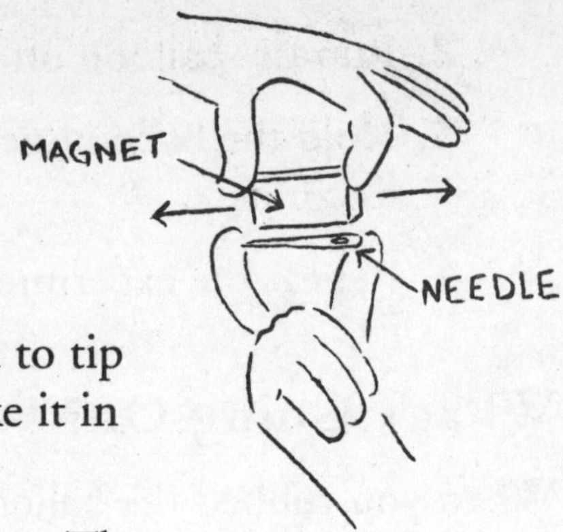

Procedure:

1. Determine which way is north.
2. Magnetize the needle by stroking from head to tip with one end of the magnet as shown. Stroke it in the same direction 40 times.
3. Tape the needle onto the matchstick as shown. The match should be longer than the needle.
4. Fill the bowl with water. Gently place the match, needle side up, on the surface of the water. It should float. Your homemade compass should immediately swing around until it points north.

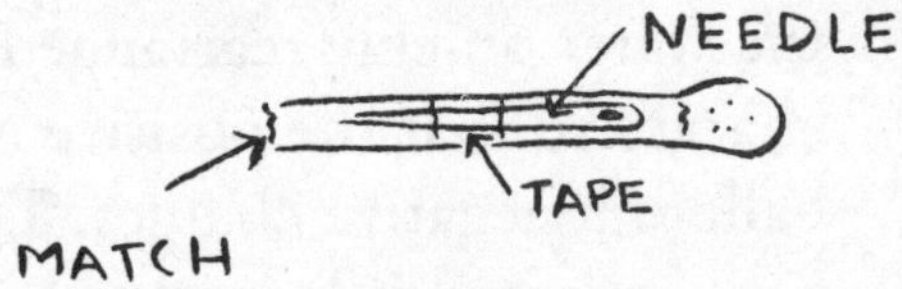

What's Going On?

A compass needle is pulled by the natural magnet inside the Earth. Just as the pull of the bar magnet is strongest at its ends, or poles, the Earth's strongest pull is at its North and South Poles. Because the United States is in the northern hemisphere, the needle of your homemade compass points north. You magnetized the needle by rearranging it internally. The steel that makes up the needle is like numerous crystals, each pointing in a different direction. By stroking them with the magnet, you reorganized them to point in one direction.

Want to Do More?

If you have a store-bought compass, use it to identify north. On a paper plate, draw a compass dial showing north, south, east and west. Place the dial underneath a bowl of water. How does your homemade compass compare with this compass?

Six-Minute Science
Dancing Paper Clip

Background:

Touch a magnet to a paper clip, and you can feel the pull. But where does the magnetic field end?

Materials:

- piece of string, about 6 inches long
- paper clip
- pencil
- tape
- bar magnet

Procedure:

1. Tie one end of the string to the paper clip. Tie the other end to the pencil. You may need to tape the knot in place so it doesn't slip.

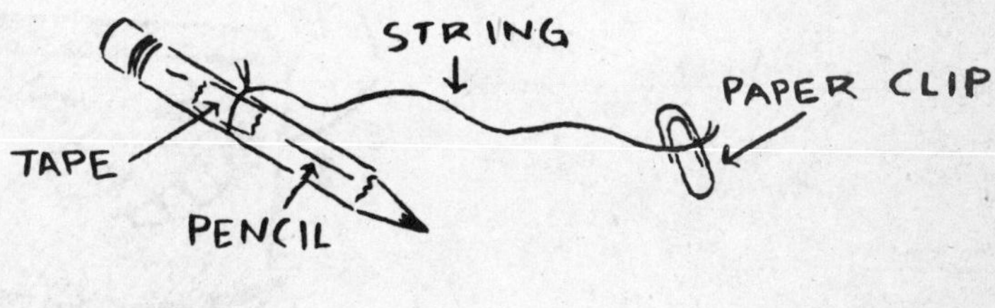

2. Hold the pencil down on a table. Let the magnet connect with the paper clip.

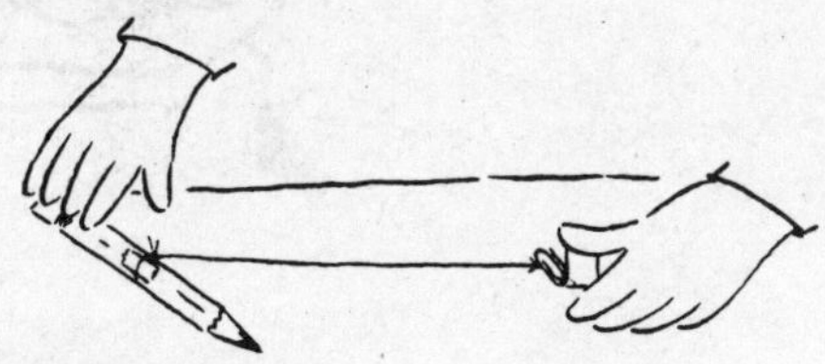

3. Lift the magnet until the string is taut. Now pull a little more until the magnet is no longer touching the paper clip.

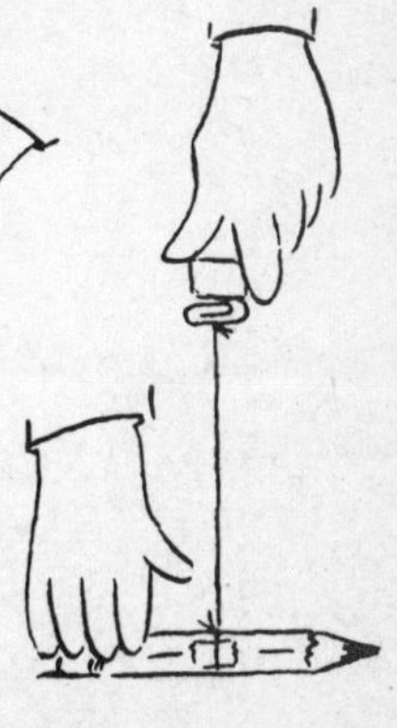

4. Remove the magnet completely, but keep it above the paper clip. If you do this gently enough, the string will stay taut and the paper clip will dance in midair.

5. Play with the magnet and paper clip. How far away can you move the magnet? What causes the paper clip to fall?

What's Going On?

Magnets have magnetic fields that extend beyond the physical magnet itself. As long as your paper clip is inside that field, it will be attracted to the magnet even if it isn't actually touching it.

Want to Do More?

Test how strong your magnet is by putting up barriers between it and the paper clip. Can you pick up the paper clip through a piece of newspaper, a plastic cup, or a glass?

FOR MORE INFORMATION

READ ALL ABOUT IT

Many more science experiment books are available covering everything from astronomy to zoology. You'll find them at your local library or bookstore. Here are just a few general books to choose from. Lots more are listed by their field of science, starting on page 102.

Cassidy, John, Paul Doherty, and Pat Murphy. *Zap Science*. Palo Alto, Calif.: Klutz Press, 1997.

Cassidy, John, and the Exploratorium. *Explorabook: A Kids' Science Museum in a Book*. Palo Alto, Calif.: Klutz Press, 1991.

Cobb, Vicki. *Chemically Active Experiments You Can Do at Home*. New York: J. B. Lippincott, 1985.

Mandell, Muriel. *Simple Weather Experiments with Everyday Materials*. New York: Sterling Publishing, 1991.

In addition, Janice VanCleave's excellent series of experiment books explore many areas of science.

GETTING OUT AND ABOUT

Check out your local nature center (there may be one at a nearby park), natural history museum, arboretum, botanical gardens, zoo, aquarium, planetarium, and university. At a nature center, you can learn about the biology of your region as well as local geology and ecology. A natural history museum may have rock displays and fossil exhibits. A museum with hands-on exhibits may have physics displays on one level and a model of a human heart on another.

AT THE LIBRARY

The library is still one of the best places to look up more information. Remember to bring along a notebook, pen or pencil, your library card, your backpack or a book bag, and change for the photocopier. Here are some research suggestions.

- Look through reference books. Encyclopedias are a good starting point. Ask the reference librarian for help.
- Search the catalog. Libraries have an entire listing of their books on computer. If the book you want is not available at your branch, speak with a librarian. You may be able to get the book through an interlibrary loan.
- Ask a librarian for help. Librarians may have suggestions about other books or magazines that may be of interest to you.

Read the science articles in your local paper. Check out the bulletin board at the local community college for lectures, presentations, or workshops you could attend. At the library, browse through books and magazines on science and nature, including *Discover* and *National Geographic*. To get you started, here is a list of books recommended by the National Science Teachers Association and the American Library Association.

BIOLOGY AND ECOLOGY

Arnosky, Jim. *Nearer Nature*. New York: Lothrop, Lee and Shepard, 1996.

Cobb, Vicki. *How to Really Fool Yourself: Illusions for All Your Senses*. New York: Wiley, 1999.

Lauber, Patricia. *Summer of Fire: Yellowstone 1988*. New York: Orchard Books, 1991.

Ross, Michael Elsohn. *Bird Watching with Margaret Morse Nice*. Minneapolis, Minn.: Carolrhoda, 1997.

Scott, Michael. *Ecology*. New York: Oxford, 1996.

Simon, Seymour. *The Brain: Our Nervous System*. New York: Morrow Junior Books, 1997.

GEOLOGY AND METEOROLOGY

Elsom, Derek. *Weather Explained: A Beginner's Guide to the Elements*. New York: Holt, 1997.

Kahl, Jonathan D. W. *Weather Watch: Forecasting the Weather*. Minneapolis, Minn.: Lerner, 1996.

Lasky, Kathryn. *Surtsey: The Newest Place on Earth*. New York: Hyperion, 1994.

Lauber, Patricia. *Living with Dinosaurs*. New York.: Aladdin Paperbacks, 1991.

Lauber, Patricia. *Volcano: The Eruption and Healing of Mount St. Helens*. New York.: Aladdin Paperbacks, 1993.

Walker, Sally M. *Earthquakes*. Minneapolis, Minn.: Carolrhoda, 1997.

CHEMISTRY AND PHYSICS

Fitzgerald, Karen. *The Story of Oxygen*. New York: Watts/Grolier, 1995.

Gonick, Larry. *The Cartoon Guide to Physics*. New York: Harper Perennial, 1991.

Maurer, Richard. *Nova Space Explorers Guide: Where to Go and What to See*. New York: Crown, 1991.

Ride, Sally. *To Space and Back.* New York.: Lothrop, Lee and Shepard, 1986.

Scott, Elaine. *Close Encounters: Exploring the Universe with the Hubble Space Telescope.* New York: Hyperion, 1998.

Skurzynski, Gloria. *Waves: The Electromagnetic Universe.* Washington, DC: National Geographic, 1995.

Wick, Walter. *Walter Wick's Optical Tricks.* New York: Cartwheel Books, 1998.

MISCELLANEOUS

Ash, Russell. *Incredible Comparisons.* London: DK Publishing, 1995.

Jackson, Donna M. *Bone Detectives: How Forensic Anthropologists Solve Crimes and Uncover Mysteries of the Dead.* New York: Little, Brown, 1996.

Johnson, Rebecca L. *Science on the Ice: An Antarctic Journal.* Minneapolis, Minn.: Lerner, 1996.

Macaulay, David. *The New Way Things Work.* Boston: Houghton Mifflin, 1998.

ON THE INTERNET

Many government agencies, national organizations, and museums post information on their Web sites. If you don't have access to the Web, contact the organizations by phone or mail. Get permission from a parent before you make a long-distance call.

Most of the Web sites on pages 106–109 don't post information about their science projects, so you'll have to dig a little deeper. If you know what you're looking for, you may be able to find a related header on the site's home page.

If you can't find the right button or link, or if you're not sure how to find what you're looking for, try these Web-surfing methods.

- Do a search of the Web site, if this feature is offered. Identify key words on the topic that interests you. For example, if you are on the National Weather Service's site and want to find out about recent hurricanes in the Atlantic Ocean, your key words could be "hurricanes" and "Atlantic." Type in the words and click on the button, or hit the Return key on your keyboard.
- Scan the news section (sometimes called News and Information or What's New) on the home page for stories related to the subject in which you're interested. This section outlines the latest goings-on in the organization's research.
- Check out links to other sites. A page on solar physics on NASA's site (www.nasa.gov) may have links to other research sites, usually belonging to a university.
- Consider subscribing to a listserve. Some organizations provide weekly E-mailings of information. If you have a family E-mail account, and if your parents agree this is a good idea, you may enjoy getting updates on the topics that interest you.

The Internet is a powerful way of gathering information, but it also can be a hazardous one. Get permission from a responsible adult before you log on. Unless your family has an unlimited-use account, you are charged by the minute for the amount of time you spend on-line, so keep your eye on the clock. If you're doing a large search, make sure you have someone else's help. It's easy to get lost on the information superhighway.

Also, don't believe every single thing you read. Anyone with a computer and a modem can put up whatever information he or she wants without having to verify the facts. Information posted on an official, government- or university-sponsored site usually is more reliable than information posted on a site put up by someone you've never heard of. If you're not sure about something you read on the Internet, go to the library and double-check it in a reference book or other published source.

GENERAL INFORMATION

American Museum of Natural History
Central Park West at West 79th St.
New York, NY 10024
(212) 769-5100
☛ **http://www.amnh.org**

The Computer Museum
Boston, MA
☛ **http://www.tcm.org**

Discovery Channel Online
☛ **http://www.discovery.com**

The Exploratorium
San Francisco, CA
☛ **http://www.exploratorium.org**

The Museum of Science
Boston, MA
☛ **http://www.mos.org**

National Academy of Sciences
Washington, DC
☛ **http://www.nas.edu**

National Museum of Natural History
Smithsonian Institution
Washington, DC 20560
(202) 357-2700
☛ **http://www.si.edu**

National Science Foundation
Arlington, VA
☛ **http://www.nsf.gov**

National Science Teachers Association
Arlington, VA
☛ **http://www.nsta.org**

BIOLOGY AND ECOLOGY

Audubon Society
☛ **http://www.audubon/org**

National Park Service
☛ **http://www.nps.gov**

National Wildlife Federation
☛ **http://www.nwf.org**

The Nature Conservancy
☛ **http://www.tnc.org**

Sierra Club
☛ **http://www.sierraclub.org**

U.S. Department of Agriculture
Agriculture Research Service
Room 340A, Administration Building
Washington, DC 20250
☛ **http://www.ars.usda.gov**

USDA Forest Service
Research Division
Sidney R. Yates Building
201 14th St. SW
Washington, DC 20250
☛ **http://www.fs.fed.us/research**

World Wildlife Fund
☛ **http://www.worldwildlife.org**

GEOLOGY AND METEOROLOGY

American Meteorological Society
45 Beacon St.
Boston, MA 02108
(617) 227-2425
☛ **http://www.ametsoc.org/ams**

Bureau of Land Management
☛ **http://www.blm.gov**

National Oceanic and Atmospheric Administration
U.S. Department of Commerce
☛ **http://www.noaa.gov**

National Weather Service Forecast Office
1325 East-West Hwy.
Silver Spring, MD 20910
(301) 713-0622
☛ **http://www.nws.noaa.gov**

U.S. Geological Survey
12201 Sunrise Valley Dr.
Mail Stop 119
Reston, VA 20192
(703) 648-4000
☛ **http://www.usgs.gov**

CHEMISTRY AND PHYSICS

American Chemical Society
☛ **http://www.acs.org**

American Physical Society
☛ **http://www.aps.org**

National Aeronautics and Space Administration
300 "E" St. SW
Washington, DC 20546
☛ **http://www.nasa.gov**

GLOSSARY

Air resistance: The force created by air pushing at an object that is moving through it.

AIR RESISTANCE

Atom: The smallest particle of matter, atoms are the building blocks of all matter. Atoms are made up of electrons, protons, and neutrons.

Bedrock: The solid rock underneath the Earth's soil, clay, sand, and gravel.

Chemosynthesis: The process by which chemicals are changed into energy.

Circuit: A complete path around which an electric current can flow.

Climate: The meteorological, or weather, conditions that remain in an area over time.

Conductor: Any material that allows electricity to pass through it.

Control group: In an experiment, the group that is not exposed to the changing variable. *See* Variable.

Controlled experiment: *See* Control group.

Convection: The movements in gases and liquids caused by warm substances rising, then cooling and falling.

Earth: The Earth is made of three principal layers: the outermost solid layer, called the crust; the mantle; and the liquid outer core and solid inner core.

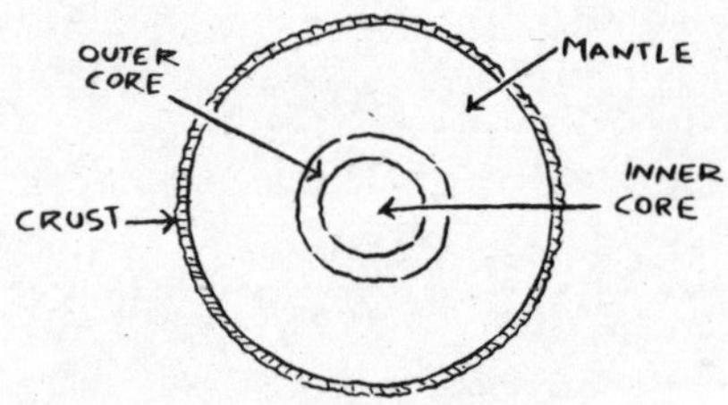

EARTH

Ecosystem: Areas that provide space, nutrients, air, and water for living creatures.

Electron: The negatively charged part of an atom.

Epidemic: An outbreak of disease.

Erosion: The wearing away of land by natural forces such as rain, wind, and ice.

Friction: The force that resists motion when one surface comes in contact with another surface, causing the two surfaces to stick together.

Gravity: The force that pulls any two objects together. The Earth pulls everything down toward its center.

Habitat: The area or type of environment that is the normal home for an organism.

Hypothesis: An educated guess or prediction about what may happen in an experiment.

Inertia: The force that resists change in movement. Things at rest will stay at rest, and things that are moving will keep moving unless another force comes into play.

Insulator: Any material that will not allow electricity to pass through it.

Matter: Any substance that takes up space, has weight, and can be perceived by the senses.

Neutron: A neutral piece of an atom that stays in the atom's center, the nucleus.

Photosynthesis: The process by which plants combine light with water to create energy used to grow.

Precipitation: Rain, snow, sleet, or hail.

PRECIPITATION

Proton: A positively charged part of an atom.

Repel: To push apart.

Variable: The object or group in an experiment that is changed so that researchers can observe the effect the variable has on the rest of the experiment. Generally, only one object is changed at a time; the rest serve as controls. *See* Control group.

Water vapor: Forms of gaseous water, including steam, fog, and ocean mist.

INDEX